AFTER AESOP

AFTER AESOP

Improvisations on Aesop's Fables

Steven Carter

Hamilton Books
A member of
The Rowman & Littlefield Publishing Group
Lanham · Boulder · New York · Toronto · Plymouth, UK

Copyright © 2010 by
Hamilton Books
4501 Forbes Boulevard
Suite 200
Lanham, Maryland 20706
Hamilton Books Acquisitions Department (301) 459-3366

Estover Road
Plymouth PL6 7PY
United Kingdom

Library of Congress Control Number: 2010923893
ISBN: 978-0-7618-5147-9 (paperback : alk. paper)
eISBN: 978-0-7618-5148-6

I am moved by fancies that are curled
Around these images, and cling:
The notion of some infinitely gentle
Infinitely suffering thing . . .

—*T.S. Eliot*

Acknowledgments

In what follows I've consulted translations by Olivia and Robert Temple (*Aesop: the Complete Fables* [London: Penguin, 1998]); Laura Gibbs (*Aesop's Fables* [London: Oxford University Press, 2002]); and George Fyler Townsend (*Aesop's Fables: Complete, Original Translation from* Greek [Forgotten Books, 2007]). The "improvisations" of this volume are, of course, original.

Many thanks as always to my formatting editor Dorothy Albritton, and to Samantha Kirk of the Rowman & Littlefield Publishing Group.

Aesop's Fables or Aesopica refers to a collection of fables attributed to Aesop (620-560 BC), a story-teller who lived in ancient Greece. Aesop's Fables have become a blanket term for collections of brief fables, usually involving personified animals. The fables remain a popular choice for moral education of children today. Many stories included in Aesop's Fables, such as The Fox and the Grapes (from which the idiom "sour grapes" was derived), The Tortoise and the Hare, The North Wind and the Sun, and The Boy Who Cried Wolf, are well-known throughout the world.

—from Wikipedia.org

Aesop, known only for the genre of fables ascribed to him, was by tradition a slave who was a contemporary of Croesus and Pesistratus in the mid-sixth century BC in ancient Greece. The various collections under the rubric "Aesop's Fables" are still taught as moral lessons and used as subjects for various entertainments, especially children's plays and cartoons. Aesop's Fables includes a compilation of tales from various sources, many of which originated with authors who lived long before Aesop. Socrates was thought to have spent his time turning Aesop's fables into verse while he was in prison. Demetrius Phalereus, another Greek philosopher, made the first collection of these fables around 300 BC. This was later translated into Latin by Phaedrus, a slave himself, around 25 BC. The fables from these two collections were soon brought together and eventually translated into Greek by Babrius around 230 AD. Many additional fables were included, and the collection was in turn translated into Arabic and Hebrew, further enriched by additional fables from these cultures.

—from Wikipedia.org

The ass and the magic potion

An ass, weary of turning a millstone around and around, pretended to have an attack of epilepsy in order to get some rest. Its owner summoned an apothecary, who said,

"I have a magic potion that you can administer to your ass. He'll be up and around in no time!"

But when the owner administered the potion, it didn't agree with the ass, and the poor creature died!

Even an ass should know that epilepsy is a disease, not a cure.

The farmer, the Cyclops, and the gold

In the land of the Cyclops, where Odysseus and his crew once visited, there was a prosperous farmer who lived with his wife and sons amid rich fields of wheat and barley. In time, however, the farmer's fortunes changed, the rains did not come, and he fell into despair. Deciding to kill himself, he took his sword into the fields, whereupon he happened upon a cache of gold left behind by a passing Cyclops. He threw down the sword, stuffed the gold in his pockets, and went home full of joy.

Soon thereafter the Cyclops returned for his gold. Seeing that it was missing, he fell into despair, picked up the sword left by the farmer, plunged it into his breast, and fell dead!

If you don't keep an eye on your money, you deserve what befalls you.

Zeus and the potsherds

Zeus decided to write down the sins of individual men on potsherds [broken pieces of pottery] and directed Hermes to put them in a box. Then, before sorting through them at random to determine punishment, he asked the other gods to bid on which sins would be the most and the least offensive.

There's a bid for every potsherd.

The partridge and the cocks

A man caught a partridge and brought it home. When he put it in the same pen with his cocks, they pecked and tormented her, until she despaired at being treated as an inferior member of a different race.

Then she noticed that the cocks also pecked and tormented one another.

She said to herself,

"What a relief! These inferior cocks have no mercy on each other either!"

1. Prejudice is a double-edged sword held by the blade.
2. You can have your cake of political correctness and eat it too.

The pregnant woman and the bed

A woman who was about to give birth lay on the ground moaning and groaning. Her husband offered to put her in bed, but she said, "My dear, it hardly makes sense that my suffering should end in the very place where it was conceived!"

Just because you make your bed doesn't mean you have to lie in it.

The fisherman and the stranger

A fisherman cast his nets across a river, damming it up. Then he beat on the water, so that the fish would become afraid and swim into the net. A stranger appeared and said to the fisherman,

"If you keep beating the water, it'll become muddied, and we who live here won't be able to drink."

But the fisherman said,

"If I stop beating the water, I'll go hungry."

To die of thirst or of hunger, what does it matter?

The rooster and the pearl

A rooster, pecking about for food in a heap of dung, came upon a pearl.

"How beautiful you are," he exclaimed, turning it in the light. "If I were human, I'd put you in a ring or on a necklace; but I'm more interested in finding food in this dung heap than I am in you!"

And the rooster threw the pearl away.

Pearls before swine are one thing, pearls before roosters quite another.

The bald man and the wig

A bald man donned a wig made of some of the hair of his father and grandfather who, as it happened, had plenty to give him. Riding his horse to town, he strutted and preened before his friends in the agora.

"Look at that!" one man said. "Our bald friend has sprouted hair!"

"Apparently so," marveled another. "Why, it's a miracle!"

Now the word "miracle" caught the attention of the gods who, impatient with the man's conceit, sent a great wind to blow through the town. The wig blew off, and the gods and the townspeople were mightily amused at the bald man's expense.

. . . But next time you see a bald man, don't laugh; he may be a hair apparent.

The young fox and the Oracle

Some foxes came down to the shore of a river to drink. They saw a calm pool on the other shore where it was safe, but the current was so strong that they became afraid and stayed where they were.

A young fox was anxious to show the rest of the foxes how courageous he was, and so he jumped in, but was swept downstream by the current.

"Wait!" the other foxes called from their shore. "Show us how we can find a safe place to cross the river so that we may drink from the pool!" But the fox called back to them bravely,

"Not now, my friends! I've a question to ask of the Oracle!"

And he disappeared around a bend.

Downstream, the Oracle saw the corpse of the young fox float by. Even though she hadn't been asked a question, she sighed in answer,

"Ah, little friend, you should've used a bridge!"

Sometimes it's better to cross your bridges whether you come to them or not.

The boy and the tripe

At a sacrificial ritual, a boy stuffed himself to the bursting point with beef tripe. When he came home he complained to his mother of a bad bellyache.

"I'm going to spew forth all my guts!" he wailed.

The mother comforted him,

"No, you won't, my boy! Those are merely the guts of the sacrificial bull you're puking up."

It takes more guts than we have to eat tripe.

The hungry fox

A hungry fox, spotting some bread and meat that shepherds had cached in the hollow of a tree, crawled in and ate all the food. But his stomach became so swollen that he couldn't get out of the hollow, and he cried for help. In time another fox happened by and said,

"Don't worry, my friend. Wait until you're hungry again and your stomach has shrunk, and you can leave the same way you got in!"

The trapped fox said, "But then I'll have no bread and meat to eat."

"You're a damn fool," said the other, and went on his way.

If you must think, think on an empty stomach.

The monkey and the fox

When a monkey was elected king of the animals, a jealous fox decided to lay a trap for him. He put a piece of meat in the trap and told the monkey that there was a treasure there for the taking. The hungry monkey-king, who lacked self-control, went for the meat and fell into the trap. When he complained that the fox had tricked him, the fox said,

"Look at you! You'd reign over all the animals, yet you can't even reign over yourself!"

To reign over all the animals, a wise king should know what hunger feels like.

The merchant and the statue of Hermes

A man of the country carved a wooden statue of the god Hermes and carried it to the market to offer it for sale, but no buyer came along. So the man began telling the crowd that he was selling a god that would be of great help around the house and in the fields. A farmer heard these words and said to the merchant,

"Friend, we aren't as foolish as you suppose. If the wooden god is so helpful around the house and in the fields, why are you selling him instead of using him yourself?"

"Ah, but I *am* using him," the merchant assured the farmer. "I'm just giving him a little help, for you know what they say, 'The gods help those who help the gods!'"

The farmer bought the statue.

Sometimes it's better to get it backward.

The fisherman and the giant octopus

A fisherman spotted a giant octopus floating on the surface of the sea near his boat. He said,

"I must beware the deadly tentacles of this octopus by all means; but if I can just grab him by the balls, I'll yank him out of the water and my family will eat for many days and nights."

But in reaching far over the side of his boat for the under-belly of the octopus, the fisherman lost his balance, fell in the water, and drowned!

By all means beware the deadly testicles of the giant octopus.

The farmer and the eagle

In the ancient days, an old farmer, known far and wide for dishonesty and meanness of heart, caught an eagle in the fields. He clipped its wings and released it into the barnyard to live in shame and humiliation with his poultry, who, of course, mocked it.

Then another man came along and bought the eagle. Taking pity on the great bird, he rubbed its wings with myrrh until they grew again. And the eagle soared into the air as before.

Soon the eagle spotted a hare, swooped down, caught it, and decided to offer it to the man who had bought him as a gift. A fox who saw what had happened said, "My friend, you shouldn't give the hare to this man. You should give it to the old farmer to deter him from catching you and clipping your wings again."

The eagle sought out the farmer and offered the hare to him. The farmer took the hare, clipped the eagle's wings again, and put him back in the barnyard, where the eagle lived in shame and humiliation till the end of his days.

1. *Deterrence doesn't always work . . . in the barnyard and in many other places.*
2. *If you don't want your wings clipped, learn the difference between deterrence and appeasement.*

Hermes and the man who made sacrifices

There was a man who spent a great deal of money making sacrifices to Hermes, the messenger-god. In time Hermes made an appearance and told him, "If I were you, I'd stop throwing away so much money on me; spend your wealth on your wife and sons before you go broke."

Thus the man gave up his custom of sacrifices altogether. Months went by, and Hermes appeared again, saying, "Well, my friend, I didn't mean for you to forego making sacrifices altogether! Surely you can offer up a small portion of your wealth to me. Now I see you revealed in your true colors as a cheapskate!"

Beware gods bearing mixed messages.

The debtor, the creditor, and the enchanted sow

When a creditor demanded that a debtor pay his debt, the debtor said he couldn't do so; instead he offered to sell his sow, which he claimed was enchanted, to the first man who came along. When a farmer happened by, the debtor asked if he would buy the enchanted sow, and the farmer asked if she were fertile. "Oh, yes," the debtor assured him, "During the winter festival of the Eleusinian mysteries she gave birth to males, and during the summer festival of Zeus she gave birth to females!"

"Hah!" the creditor interrupted. "This is far too fantastic. Next you'll tell him that the sow would give birth to baby goats for the god Dionysius."

The debtor thought a moment, for the creditor had given him an idea.

"No," he said to the creditor, "but she'll give birth to debtors!"

The creditor took the sow and forgave the debtor's debt.

Greed = interest charged on creditors.

The loquacious cat and the clever cock

A certain cat caught a cock in its claws.

"I'm going to eat you because you keep people awake with your infernal crowing," said the cat.

"No, no," countered the cock. "Thanks to the likes of me the farmer performs his chores on time."

"Well," said the cat, "I'm going to eat you because you live in sin with your mother and sisters."

"Yes," admitted the cock, "but that's how chickens provide eggs for the farmer."

So it went, accusation after accusation, justification after justification, until the cat, weakened with hunger, fainted dead away and the cock escaped to live another day.

Don't talk with your mouth empty.

The fox and the henhouse

A fox, hearing that some chickens were sick, put on a doctor's white coat, found a doctor's black bag, and visited the henhouse.

Immediately the cock guarding the henhouse threw him out.

"Go work your mischief in another henhouse!" the cock called after him.

"Congratulations," said one clever hen to the cock, "You saved us from the fox!"

"Fox?" said the astonished cock, "I thought he was a doctor!"

Even foxes don't make house calls.

The dog and Hermes

Trotting down the road one day, a terrier happened upon a statue of Hermes.

"Will you anoint me?" said the statue.

"I have no sacred oil, O Hermes," said the dog humbly, lifting his leg. "So with your permission I will anoint you in the only way I know how."

He peed on the statue and trotted on.

Take your worship where you find it.

The master, the ugly slave-girl, and Aphrodite

A certain master loved an ugly slave-girl who worked in his house. But the slave-girl wasn't satisfied to be loved, and she prayed to Aphrodite to make her beautiful so that the master would love her even more.

The presumption of the slave-girl irritated the jealous Aphrodite, who was also angry at the master for preferring the ugly slave-girl to her. And so, to take revenge on them both, the goddess granted her wish and made her beautiful! And the master, seeing that she was no longer the ugly slave-girl he loved, cast her out of his house, and lived alone to the end of his days.

Ugly, too, is in the eye of the beholder.

The dog and the reeds

A starving dog happened upon a clump of reeds growing by a river. Now, dogs don't eat reeds as a rule, but in this case he had little choice. He ate some of the reeds, then, feeling the need to relieve himself, lowered his behind on the rest. Just then one reed jabbed sharply him in the haunch, and the poor dog was obliged to find another place to do his business.

"Serves you right," the reed called after him. "It was one thing to eat my friends, quite another to try pooping on me!"

Don't shit where you feed, for it's offal business insulting the dignity of a reed.

The hungry fisherman and the small mackerel

A hungry fisherman cast his nets in the sea but caught only one small mackerel. The fish begged for its life, saying, "If you let me go I'll grow up to be a very large fish, and you can catch me then, and I'll feed you and your family for many days."

The fisherman said to the small mackerel, "If I let you go, I may never see you again, no matter how big you are when you grow up!" And he took the mackerel home, and his wife scolded him as always, and the fisherman and his family again went hungry.

A large mackerel in the sea is worth more than a small mackerel in the hand.

The old fisherman who made things difficult

Some fishermen went down to the shore each day with a drag-net, but every time they pulled it in it was filled with stones. One of the fishermen, an old man, lectured the rest, saying,

"Affliction is Joy's brother, my friends," and, "The easy life is but a pipe dream, we all know that, my friends," and "If at first you don't succeed, try again, my friends," so that the fishermen's days were filled, not just with disappointment, but with the weariness of hearing the old man's endless words.

This went on and on until the angry fishermen began to think that the old man *himself* was the cause of their misfortunes, and they threw the stones in the net at him, driving the poor fellow off!

"You see?" said one to the others. "The stones were the bounty we had sought after all!"

If at first you don't succeed, simplify, simplify.

Prometheus and the roads to freedom and slavery

Zeus asked Prometheus to make two roads for mankind, the road to freedom and the road to slavery, on condition that the roads diverge from one place. Prometheus decided to make the road to freedom long and winding, leading through dark and dangerous woods where wild beasts dwelled. Soon, however, it opened onto open country, resplendent with meadows and streams and all the good things of this earth.

As for the road to slavery, it began as a straight and easy path through beautiful country, but soon turned treacherous, leading to despair and death.

Thus the two roads presented all travelers with the greatest dilemma to be found in the world of men.

"When you come to a fork in the road, take it."

The fox and the leopard

Walking down a country road, a fox and a leopard were arguing about the nobility of their respective heritages. As they disputed the titles and distinctions of their ancestors, they came to a graveyard, whereupon the fox began to weep.

When the leopard asked what the matter was, the fox said,

"Oh, when I think of all my brave and noble ancestors asleep in this graveyard, it breaks my heart!"

Just then the earth opened up, and many dead foxes rose from the graves. They said to the leopard,

"Bah! Don't believe a word he says, the scoundrel! We, too, were scoundrels, and rogues and villains to boot!"

Why not speak ill of the dead, when you know pretty well what they would say about you.

The dull-witted acolytes

Two dull-witted acolytes met in the marketplace of Corinth every day to dispute whether the god Apollo or the god Poseidon was the greater. But the two gods, bored with the interminable palaver of the acolytes, turned deaf ears to both of them forever.

All that the quarrels of underlings accomplish is that their masters are equally unfortunate in putting up with them.

The little birds and the lonely cuckoo

Little birds were always fleeing from a lonely cuckoo. When the cuckoo asked them why, they said,

"It's a known fact that you'll soon turn into a hawk, and tear us to pieces!"

Ornithologist, heal thyself.

The cowardly man and the ravens

A cowardly man was compelled to go to war. But, upon hearing some ravens croak, he dropped his spear and sword in the road and froze trembling where he was. Then, as he proceeded a bit further, he heard the croaks again, dropped his weapons, and froze trembling where he was. This happened again and again, and the cowardly man got nowhere.

Sometimes the journey is better than the destination.

The sick man and the gods

A man fell ill with a lingering illness, and no doctor could help him. Finally he prayed to the gods, and said, "If you cure me, I'll make a votive offering to you every day of my life."

His wife said, "And where will you get the money to do that?"

"Don't you see?" the man said. "The gods will keep me alive until I can pay the debt!"

But one of the gods, overhearing the man's scheme, sent a thunderbolt and struck him dead.

1. *You can only fool some of the gods some of the time.*
2. *Better to be struck dead by a thunderbolt than die of a lingering illness.*

The pigeon and the snake

A pigeon built its nest inside a hall of justice. One day she flew off in search of food, and a snake, seeing that she was gone, raided the nest and devoured all her little ones. When the pigeon returned she began wailing at the unfair loss of her children.

A passing swallow said,

"Take heart, my dear; others of our ilk have lost their babies too!"

But the pigeon wouldn't be consoled. "Where was justice when I needed it?" she complained over and over.

If you live in a hall of justice, don't expect justice to come to you.

The hen and the cat

A hen fell ill. A cat approached and said, "I happen to be a doctor, my dear. May I examine you?"

"I'll be just fine," said the hen, "providing you fly the coop!"

Doctors can't kill you if you won't let them.

The shipwreck, the man, the ants, and Hermes

A ship sank to the bottom of the sea, taking everyone on board with it. A man on shore who witnessed the sinking claimed that the gods were unfair to sacrifice many innocent lives to destroy one or two impious men.

Just then a troop of ants happened by and bit the man on the ankle. Outraged, the man crushed every ant under his sandal.

Whereupon the god Hermes appeared, struck the man on the head with his scepter, and said, "And don't you see that the gods judge you in the same way that you judged the ants? When misfortune befalls you, my friend, look to your own faults!"

. . . Unless of course it rains on the just and the unjust alike, in which case crush all the ants you want.

The man, the sparrow, and Apollo

A man from Corinth traveled to Delphi, intent on proving that Apollo and the other gods were frauds. He concealed a sparrow in his cloak, planning to ask Apollo if the bird were dead or alive. If Apollo said that the bird was dead, the man would show him the live bird. If Apollo said that the bird was alive, the man would crush it, and show the body to Apollo.

But Apollo, seeing through the man's ruse, said, "Enough, you fool! For it depends on *you* whether the bird is dead or alive."

"Then what do I need you for?" said the man from Corinth, and he let the sparrow go.

And Apollo smiled a secret smile, for there is providence in the rise of a sparrow.

The ways of the gods are passing strange.

The man with two mistresses

A fifty-year-old man who was going gray had two mistresses, one young, one old. The older mistress was abashed that she was having an affair with a much younger man, so that, each time she came to his house, she pulled out his black hairs. For her part, the younger mistress was abashed that she was having an affair with a much older man, so that, each time she came to his house, she pulled out his white hairs.

Thus it came to pass that, plucked by both women, the man became bald.

. . . *And both mistresses loved him all the more, for everyone knows bald men are more virile than men with hair.*

Prometheus and Opportunity

Prometheus made Opportunity to be grasped from the front only; from the rear, he designed her to be almost impossible to hold onto. Thus many men, slow to act, would come to curse Opportunity for appearing in their doorway in the first place!

Don't knock Opportunity.

The eyeless man and the wolf cub

Once there was an eyeless man who took pride in recognizing all things by touch. Then, one day, someone handed him a wolf cub.

"This is a lamb," he said, "and it should be put in the fold to grow up with the other lambs!"

You don't need eyes to be blind to the truth.

The proud wolf and the pride of lions

A very large wolf tried to join a pride of lions, but the lions laughed at him. Then the wolf invoked Zeus,

"If you would only give me a mane, I, too, could be a mighty lion," he boasted.

Like the lions, Zeus laughed at the pretensions of the silly wolf.

"Accept the nature of things, my friend! You were a wolf, are a wolf, and will be a wolf every day of your life!"

In the mane, wolves puffed up with pride are lion to themselves.

The sick man, the gods, and the pirates

A man lay gravely ill, and he prayed to the gods to cure him of his sickness, saying that he would burn a hundred oxen [a hecatomb] as a votive offering. The gods decided to put his word to the test, so they cured him, saying,

"Okay, where are our oxen?" But the man had misled the gods, for he was poor, and he made one hundred oxen out of wax, and burned them on an altar, and said,

"This is the offering I promised, O gods."

For their part, the gods decided to mislead the man.

"Go to the seashore," they told him, "and it will result in one thousand drachmas for you." The man went to the seashore, where he was captured by pirates. The pirates sold him into slavery, receiving one thousand drachmas for him.

Bribe the gods by all means, but make sure you're in good health.

The man, Aesop, and the bow

A man happened upon Aesop playing marbles with some children in the road. When the man laughed, telling Aesop that he was unwise to waste his time in such a frivolous manner, Aesop took out his unstrung bow and put it in the road.

"All right," he told the man, "if *you* are so wise, my friend, tell me what this signifies."

The man thought and thought, and finally confessed to be at a loss.

"If I keep the bow strung," said Aesop, "it'll eventually snap in two; but if I keep it unstrung, it'll always be ready to use."

Then the man, noticing what a beautifully-made bow it was, snatched it up and ran away!

When you come to a bow in the road, take it.

The beetle and the eagle

A beetle looked up from his dung heap and saw an eagle soaring high in the sky.

"Oh, how I wish I could be like him," he said. "Neither proper bug nor bird, I'm condemned to spend my life crawling about in a heap of filth. Well, by Zeus, it's time for a change!"

And the beetle rose into the air, trying to imitate the eagle; but soon a mighty wind came up, caught the unfortunate creature in its clutches, and dashed him to the ground, where he lay mortally injured.

"Woe is me," said the beetle. "If I could only have my dung heap once again, I'd be a happy beetle after all!"

Be it ever so humble, and we do mean humble, there's no place like home.

The farmer and the fox

A farmer decided to take revenge on a fox that had done him some damage. He caught the fox, tied a rope dipped in oil to its tail, set fire to the rope, and let the fox go. The fox ran into the fields, setting fire to the farmer's crops, and escaped safe and sound. The farmer was ruined.

"Oh!" the farmer lamented. "What a terrible turn of events! I've lost my opportunity to take revenge on that fox!"

Some people can't keep their priorities straight.

The gods and man

The gods blessed the animals with wings to fly and strong legs to run swiftly, but they made man naked. Man complained that the gods were unfair in this, but the gods said, "But we have given you the gift of speech; surely that's a greater thing than wings or the strongest legs."

"In the mouths of men speech is a blessing," man agreed. "But in the mouths of women it's a curse!"

"No," the gods said, closing their ears. "Surely no woman is as noisy as you!"

Half a curse is better than none.

The swallow and the birds who wouldn't take heed

A swallow noticed that a farmer was putting in flax seed, and he warned the other birds:

"There's trouble brewing in that field, for when the flax grows up bird-catchers will make snares of it, and you know what that means, my friends."

The other birds laughed at the swallow, so he persisted in his warning:

"Do you want your heads chopped off? Do as I am about to do, my friends, and leave this vicinity!"

But the birds still laughed, and the swallow flew off and made his nest far away from the field of flax.

In time the flax grew tall, the farmer sold it to bird-catchers, and the birds who laughed at the swallow were captured in the bird-catchers' snares and promptly beheaded.

If you would be spared the ax, stay away from fields of flax.

The man, the lion, and the statue

A man and a lion were arguing about which one was the stronger. Just then they passed a statue of a man strangling a lion.

"You see?" said the man proudly. "We're stronger than you."

"Hah!" replied the lion. "If lions made statues, you'd see plenty of men in their clutches."

"But you don't understand," said the man, "I happen to know that it *was* a lion who made the statue. A lion of truth, I might add!"

Then the lion, tired of the man's boasting, strangled him.

A wise philosopher[1] said, "We have art so that we may not perish from the truth."

_____

1. Nietzsche.

The rooster who founded a religion

A rooster decided to found a religion, with him as the exalted leader, of course. All the animals came to hear him preach, including the cats. When the rooster traveled from town to town to spread his gospel, he asked the cats to carry him on a litter, which the cats were very happy to do.

But a god appeared to the rooster and warned, "Look carefully at the faces of these worshippers. They're less interested in carrying you than in eating you!"

"I don't believe so," the rooster said. "Let's keep moving, my furry friends!"

Sure enough, when the procession reached a deserted part of the road they were on, the cats turned on the rooster, tore him to pieces, and devoured him!

Don't judge a church by the congregation.

The man and the god fashioned from clay

A man prayed to a household god fashioned from clay to help him in his poverty, but the god did nothing, and the man's poverty became worse and worse. Angered, the man picked up the god by the legs and shattered it against the wall. But when the god's head fell off, gold coins fell out of its body!

Then the man said, "What a contrary spirit you have! When I prayed to you, you wouldn't help me. But now you give me gold coins!"

"It's *you* who have the contrary spirit, my friend," said the god. "Yes, I've given you gold coins, but look what you've done to me!"

As long as gods with feet of clay pay the bills, keep the faith.

The man and the golden statue of the lion

A man happened upon a statue of a lion made of pure gold, but was afraid to take it.

"What'll I do?" he said. "I'm divided between my desire for the lion and my cowardly nature. Is this an accident? Did some god or goddess make the lion and leave it here to tempt me? Will I be punished if I take it? And what if I *did* take it? What use would I really have for it? For you know what they say . . ."

And the statue said to the man, "Oh, stop your infernal complaining and please go away!"

The man went away, happy to leave the dilemma of the golden lion far behind him.

Peace of mind beats a statue of a golden lion every time.

The bear and the fox

A bear and a fox were traveling through a meadow. The bear boasted to the fox that he was a great lover of mankind because he never ate human carrion.

"But then, my friend," said the fox, "why do you kill living men if not to eat them?"

"You know," replied the bear, "I never looked at it that way!"

Equally as important for a bear as for a man to look out for number one.

The wolf and the ploughman

A ploughman unhitched his oxen and took them to the stream to drink. A hungry wolf, seeing this, crept up and began to lick the yoke, for it tasted of oxen. Then, inch by inch, the wolf's neck sank into the yoke and got stuck there. And the imprisoned wolf dragged the plough into the furrow.

And the ploughman was pleasantly surprised to see that the wolf, who was well known for robbing and pillaging, had decided to work for his bread after all!

Why you plough your furrow is of little importance; just plough it.

The well and the stars

A man was accustomed to enjoying the beauty of the stars every night. But one evening, gazing at the sky, he fell into a deep well. A passerby heard him moaning and groaning, and said, "What are you doing down there, friend?"

This gave the man an idea. "Why, gazing at the sky, my friend. The view is much better from here. You ought to come down and see!"

And the passerby entered the well to look at the beauty of the stars. He said,

"Truly, I never noticed how beautiful the stars were before!"

Soon another passerby happened along and said, "What are you two doing down there?" The man said, "Gazing at the sky, my friend. You ought to join us!"

The second passerby entered the well, and he, too, said that he'd never noticed how beautiful the stars were before.

This went on and on until a ladder of passersby had risen in the well, whereupon the man climbed the ladder and escaped. Alas, his adventure had robbed him of all interest in enjoying the beauty of the stars, and he went home and fell into a black mood till the end of his days.

Better to have your head in the clouds than your feet in the ground.

The frogs and the serpent-god

The frogs, tired of having no protection in their lives, asked Zeus to send a god who would take care of them. Zeus gave them a willow branch, but when the branch did nothing, the frogs climbed upon it to show contempt, and complained to Zeus once again.

Therefore Zeus, impatient with the imprecations of the frogs, sent them a serpent-god that ate them all up.

But the frogs thanked Zeus, for they felt protected and safe in the belly of the serpent-god!

Even the gods will tell you that the ways of the gods are passing strange.

The frog and the fox

A frog cried out to all the animals in the swamp,
    "I'm a doctor, and I can heal what ails you!"
    But a fox said, "How can you say that, my friend, when you can't even heal your own limp?"
    Enraged, the frog bit the fox on the leg.
    "*Now* what do you think, my friend?" demanded the frog.
    "I think that you'd make a good doctor, my friend," said the fox.

Patient, heal thyself.

The horses and the axle

Two horses were pulling a cart down a country road. As the axle creaked, they turned and said,

"Hah! It's we who do all the work and yet it's you who moans!"

"But I'm saving you the trouble of moaning," said the axle.

"We never thought of that," replied the horses, and resumed their hard work.

When it comes to brains, always put the cart before the horse.

The lion and the oxen

Three oxen were in the habit of grazing together. A lion wanted to eat them, but he could never get them by themselves. So he convinced them that each was spreading rumors about the other, and soon they shunned each other's company, and the lion was able to eat them all.

1. There's safety in numbers, providing that everyone gets along.
2. Better to be eaten up by slander than by a lion.

The priests and the ass

A roving band of priests of the goddess Demeter owned a foolish ass which carried their food and belongings. The ass was given to stopping in its tracks, so that the priests had to beat him constantly with sticks and whips. Finally the ass died, and the priests skinned it to make tambourines and drums, which, in their travels, they pounded on with the same ferocity as when the foolish ass was among the living.

When a passerby asked how they had made their musical instruments, the priests told him, adding,

"That foolish ass still hasn't learned his lesson!"

Beating a dead horse is one thing, beating a dead ass quite another.

The ox-driver and Hermes

An ox-driver took his wagon to town, but the wagon fell down a ravine. Rather than lifting a finger to solve the problem, he prayed to Hermes to help him out of his difficulty. The god appeared to him and said, "You'd better put in some effort yourself, my friend. The gods help those who help themselves!"

But the ox-driver, slothful by nature, pretended to put his hand to the wheels and to goad the oxen. Then Hermes said, "Now that's more like it, my friend!" and put the oxen and the wagon back on the road, and the ox-driver went on to town.

When the other gods saw that the wagon had made it to town, some applauded the ox-driver, but others laughed at Hermes.

You can fool all of the gods some of the time, you can fool some of the gods all of the time, but you can't fool all of the gods all of the time.

The slave and Aesop in the agora

One day in the agora a slave came up to Aesop and complained of his lot, saying that his master beat him constantly, never gave him enough to eat, and made him sleep outside in the gutter.

"I want to escape," he added, "for I'm guiltless and haven't done a thing to deserve this punishment!"

"Ah," said Aesop, raising a finger, "but now you're contemplating committing the crime of escaping from your master. If I were you, my friend, I'd think twice about that!"

And the slave went back to his master.

Unless you plan to spend the rest of your life in the gutter, think twice before accepting advice from Aesop.

The linnet and the bat

A linnet, whose cage hung next to an open window, sang all night long. A bat in the forest heard the singing and came to investigate.

"Why, my friend," he asked the linnet, "do you sing by night and not by day?"

"I have good reason," replied the linnet. "It was by daylight that my master heard me singing and put me in a cage, so now I know better."

"Ah, but you should've thought of that *before* your master caught you, you silly bird," said the bat, who was rather smug.

"Not really, my friend," said the linnet. "*You* have to work hard to earn a living, flittering and fluttering here and there every night unto exhaustion, while *I* am well fed and quite happy in my cage!"

And the bat, which had a wearisome night's hunting ahead of him, flew off; and the linnet resumed his song.

Better to be a silly bird content in a cage than a wise bat weary in the wild.

The shepherd and Zeus

A shepherd lost a lamb. He said to Zeus, "If you'll find the thief for me, I'll sacrifice a kid to you and your wife."

Then the shepherd went to the woods to look for the lamb, and came across a lion eating it for dinner!

The shepherd thought to himself for a moment; then he said to Zeus, "I've found the thief, Oh mighty Zeus, and there's the kid I promised to you and your wife."

Zeus was pleased at the sacrifice, and replaced the kid with another one; and the shepherd returned to his flock, pleased that he had put one over on the King of Olympus.

[See the moral to "The ox-driver and Hermes," above.]

The house-ferret, the handsome young man, and Aphrodite

A house-ferret [domesticated polecat] fell in love with a handsome young man, and prayed to Aphrodite to change her into a beautiful young woman. After giving it some thought, the goddess reluctantly granted her wish, for she was attracted to the handsome young man herself.

Then, one night in their bedchamber, the transformed girl saw a rat, forgot what the goddess had done for her, and jumped out of bed to eat it. Angry at the girl's ingratitude, Aphrodite changed her back into a house-ferret.

Then the handsome young man begged the goddess to change *him* into a house-ferret, so that he might live happily ever after with the creature he'd grown to love. Aphrodite, even angrier that he preferred a house-ferret to her, granted his wish.

Punishment is its own reward.

The old man and Death

An old man chopped a pile of wood. When he saw how heavy the wood would be to carry, he called upon Death. When Death appeared, he asked the old man why he'd summoned him.

"For you to help me pick up my burden," the old man said.

And Death took the old man.

The old man's ghost said to Death, "But why didn't you help me to pick up my burden?"

Death said, "Oh, I beg your pardon! I thought you said, 'Put down my burden.'"

Be careful what you don't wish for.

The ploughman and the dogs

A ploughman couldn't leave his farm to go into the village for food, due to prolonged icy weather. First he ate his sheep, then, as the bad weather continued, he ate his goats. Then he turned to his oxen, whereupon the farm dogs said to each other,

"Ah, well, we're safe, for surely he won't eat dog!"

There's no accounting for some people's taste.

The serpent and the ploughman

A serpent bit the son of a ploughman, killing the young boy. The ploughman, eager for revenge, attempted to kill the serpent with an axe, but when the serpent stuck its head out of its hole, and the ploughman swung his axe, he cleaved a boulder in two instead.

Then the ploughman tried to make peace with the serpent, lest it bite him too.

But the serpent said, "There can be no peace between us, because I've witnessed the gouge you made in the rock, and you have witnessed the tomb I made for your child."

Peace between warring parties has nothing to do with peace, everything to do with war.

The old man, the sons, and the vineyard

An old man, the owner of a poor vineyard, fell ill. As he wanted his sons to know the meaning of work before he died, he said,

"I want you to look in the vineyard for a treasure and tell me when you find it." And the sons hoed and hoed the earth, but they found no treasure. When they told their father of their disappointment he said,

"Don't you see what's happened, my boys? You've made the earth richer by tending it thus, and now our little crop will finally prosper. That's the treasure I spoke of!"

But the sons weren't satisfied, and when the father died they let the vineyard go to seed; and they packed up and moved to town where they became greedy merchants, prospered, and lived happily ever after!

The road to heaven is paved with bad intentions.

The ass and the tanner

An ass complained to Zeus that his master, a gardener, worked him too hard and gave him too little to eat. Zeus ordered Hermes to give the ass to a potter, but the ass complained that he, too, worked him too hard. This went on until Zeus lost patience with the ass and told Hermes to give the ass to a tanner, who cut his throat and skinned him.

When asking the gods for favors, don't be a bloody ass.

The ploughman and the tree

A ploughman of sour disposition decided to cut down a tree in the middle of his fields. He began to chop at it with an axe, but the cicadas and linnets who lived in the tree pleaded with him, saying that if he spared their home they'd charm him with their music. But the ploughman scorned them, and struck the tree again, until all at once his axe revealed a hive of bees and a rich store of honey!

From then on the ploughman honored the tree and tended it well.

Better honey than vinegar, even for ploughmen.

The ploughman and the Goddess of Chance

A ploughman happened upon a sack of gold coins in his fields. Overjoyed, he graced the image of Mother Earth with a garland in gratitude. But the Goddess of Chance appeared and said, "My friend, why do you so grace Mother Earth, when it was I who left the gold coins in your field? If the gold coins should pass from you, I know whom you will blame!"

The man pondered these words, and graced the image of the Goddess of Chance with a garland as well. And he kept the gold, left the fields, and retired to a villa on the French Riviera.

Fortune favors those who hedge their bets.

The farmer's ears and the honey

The ears of a farmer complained that the mouth was much better off than they were, because the mouth enjoyed honey and they did not. Thus the farmer asked Zeus to change the nature of things by allowing him to put honey in his ears rather than his mouth. And Zeus granted his wish.

Whereupon the honey that the farmer put into his ears flowed into his head, and he died!

Better honey in the mouth than honey in the horn.

The kindly father, the apple tree, and the quarrelsome sons

A kindly father had five quarrelsome sons. No matter what he said, they ignored him and continued quarreling. Then he had an idea. He chopped an apple tree into bundles of sticks, handed each son a bundle, and told them to break it up. When they could not, he broke the bundles into sticks, and the five sons broke them with ease.

"You see?" said the kindly father. "If you stay together like the bundles, you'll be hard to defeat. But if you're divided like the sticks, your enemies will triumph!"

But the quarrelsome sons ignored the father's words and began to beat each other about the head and shoulders with the sticks.

The apple falls far from the tree.

The old woman, the doctor, and the judge

An old woman whose eyes were failing sent for a doctor. The doctor put unguent on her eyes, and when her eyes were closed with the unguent, he stole pieces of her furniture one at a time. When the treatments were completed, the woman refused to pay the doctor, complaining that her eyes were worse than ever. "Before you came, I could see all my furniture," she told the doctor, "but now I can't see any of it at all!"

The doctor and the old woman went before a judge. The doctor defended himself, saying, "I didn't see the thief who took her furniture!"

The judge thought about these words for a moment. Then he said to the doctor,

"I order you to apply the unguent to yourself, for it's clear that your eyes, too, are failing."

Even doctors get a dose of their own medicine, though not often.

The dutiful wife and the drunken husband

A dutiful wife was burdened with a drunken husband. To teach him a lesson, she waited until he was dead drunk one night, then threw him over her shoulder, carried him to the cemetery, and locked him in a mausoleum. The next day she returned and pounded on the door.

"Who is it?" said the husband, who was still drunk from the night before.

"It is the one who brings food for the dead," the wife said.

"Food?" said the man. "My God, I want drink, not food."

Thus it was clear to the dutiful wife that the husband would never change.

And she brought more for the husband to drink, and left him to rot in the mausoleum.

Always leave your revenge with a little kindness.

The widow and the servant-girls

Once there was a mean-spirited widow who had three servant-girls. She worked them very hard, rousting them out of bed in the morning when the cock crew. Finally the girls, exhausted from their labors, decided to kill the cock, for they believed it was he who caused their suffering by waking the widow at dawn. But after they had carried out their plan, and the cock no longer sounded the hour, the widow got up before dark and rousted the girls even earlier than before.

Thus it was that the three servant-girls killed the mean-spirited widow and got plenty of sleep from then on.

Never be afraid to eliminate the middleman.

The widow and the magic hen

A certain widow owned a magic hen that laid twenty eggs a day. Then she decided that if she fed the hen more barley, it would lay even more eggs, and she'd grow rich. But when the widow fed the hen more barley, it stopped laying eggs, and began laying bushels and bushels of barley each day instead! And she took the barley to market and grew twice as rich on the bushels as she once hoped to on the eggs.

It pays to diversify.

The prophetic sorceress

Once there was a sorceress who made her living selling magic potions to appease the wrath of the gods. But a jealous neighbor charged her with making changes in religion, and she was tried and found guilty of the allegations, although they were false. And when, on the day of her execution, she was asked if she wished to offer an apology, she said, "I apologize for nothing! Mark my words, my friends; a distant time will come when, bereft of my potions, the entire world will suffer the wrath of the gods!"

The woman was true to her words, for that era became the Inquisition.

Give the same lie enough time and it becomes a different truth.

The heifer and the ox

A heifer saw an ox hard at work in the fields, and said,

"Dear ox, I'm truly sorry for the burdens you carry." Just then a company of religious zealots happened by, and decided to roast the heifer in sacrifice to the gods. And the ox said to the heifer,

"Ah, dear heifer, it seems that you, not I, was meant to be sacrificed!"

"Yes," the heifer agreed, "but I still prefer my fate to yours!"

Better to be a heifer than an ox, even on the spit.

The hunter, the woodcutter, and the lion

A hunter asked a woodcutter to help him look for the tracks of a lion. The woodcutter said, "I'll do better than that; I'll take you to the actual lion."

Just then the lion pounced from behind a tree, devoured the woodcutter, and ran off.

Sometimes reading a map is more fun than actually going there.

The young sow and the lambs

A young sow began grazing with a flock of sheep. When the shepherd caught her she began to squeal, whereupon the lambs said to her, "What a fuss you make! *We* don't squeal up a storm when the shepherd catches us!"

"Yes," said the young sow. "But all the shepherd wants from you is your wool. In my case it's skin that he's after!"

"No, no," the lambs disagreed. "This shepherd is always hungry; he cares more about making meals of us than he does about what his wife makes from our wool!"

You might as well stop squealing, for you can't make a silk purse from a sow's ear or from a lamb's wool.

The whales, the dolphins, and the magic minnow

The dolphins and the whales entered into battle. As the fight went on and on, a magic minnow came to the surface of the sea and tried to get them to stop. But the dolphins and the whales laughed at him.

"How dare *you*, of all fish in the sea, interfere in our titanic battle? Go back to where you came from, you mite!"

And the minnow, angered at this insult, changed into a gigantic sea-serpent, and devoured all the whales and the dolphins in one swallow!

There's more than one way to broker a peace.

Diogenes and the bald man

The Cynic Diogenes carried a lantern through the streets of Athens at high noon, looking for an honest man. In the agora he came upon a bald man, who insulted him.

Diogenes replied, "Friend, let me commend the common sense of the hairs which have left your hideous skull."

The bald man came back, "And *I* pity the words which leave your tongue to go unheeded in the agora!"

. . . *Thus Diogenes found his honest man.*

The oak trees and Zeus

The oak trees complained to Zeus that their lives meant nothing, since they grew up only to be felled by the axe. But Zeus replied,

"It's your own fault, my friends. You produce the wood that makes the axe, and you're very useful to man in other ways!"

The oak trees said,

"That may be true; but if you were more useful to those who dwell here on earth, many more would pay homage to you!"

And Zeus was well rebuked.

Take your wisdom where you find it, even from oak trees.

Diogenes, the old woman, and the soup

Diogenes went on a journey, taking his barrel[2] with him. He became hungry, and went to a farmhouse, where an old woman fed him good, hot soup. Just then another traveler happened by, and the old woman gave him good, hot soup; and another, and another.

Finally Diogenes said to her,

"I won't thank you, for it's clear to me that you're driven to do what you do by a demon over which you have no control!"

And the woman said,

"But, sir, what does it matter *why* I give soup to hungry strangers, so long as I am happy to do so?"

And Diogenes, moved by her words, when he arrived back home also began giving good, hot soup to hungry travelers.

One good tureen deserves another.

---

2. Diogenes the Cynic, a disciple of Socrates, was reputed to have lived in a barrel, sometimes called a tub in translation.

The woodcutters and the pine tree

Some woodcutters were splitting a pine tree. Their work was made much easier by the wedges made of its wood which they drove into the tree. And the pine tree lamented,

"It's not the axe that hurts me as much as the wedges, for they are part of me!"

It's a known fact that pine trees are their own worst enemy.

The silver fir tree and the bramble

A silver fir tree and a bramble were arguing. The silver fir boasted,

"I'm beautiful, tall, and very valuable to the men who use my wood to make decks and masts of ships of the Athenian navy that roam the seas."

The bramble replied,

"Ah, my friend, when you remember the saws and axes that cut you, you'll be damn sorry you weren't born a bramble!"

Brambles, which don't have an opportunity to join the navy and see the world, have a limited view of things.

The kid, the wolf, and the roof of the house

A kid, chased by a wolf, jumped on top of the roof of a house and began to laugh and jeer at the wolf. The wolf said,

"Hah! It's not you, my little friend, but your position of safety that mocks me!" But the roof said to the wolf,

"Not me, my friend! I've much better sense than to mock a wolf!"

"Really?" said the kid, turning to the roof. "What do you know anyway? You're nothing but the stupid roof of a house!"

Then the roof, angered by the kid's ill-advised words, huffed and puffed and shook him off, whereupon the kid was caught and eaten by the wolf!

Mockery will get you nowhere, even standing on the roof of a house.

Hermes and the sculptor

Hermes wished to know how men on earth thought of him, and so he put on a disguise and visited a sculptor who made statues of the gods. He pointed to a statue of Zeus and asked the sculptor, "How much for that one?"

"Twenty drachmas," the sculptor replied.

Then he pointed to a statue of Athena: "How much for that one?"

"Thirty drachmas," the sculptor replied.

Then he pointed to a statue of himself.

"One hundred drachmas," said the sculptor, "for Hermes is the most beautiful of gods."

"But that's too much!" Hermes exclaimed before he knew what he was saying.

"It's quite odd that you should say that, sir," said the sculptor. "For it's very well known that Hermes is the god of profit-making!"

Only a penny-pincher puts his vanity second.

The wolf and the lamb

A wolf chased a lamb that had fallen behind the flock. The lamb said to the wolf,

"If you'll play the flute I'll dance for you; *then* you can eat me." The wolf played the flute, and the lamb danced, but just then three hunters happened by, and chased the wolf away. And the wolf said over his shoulder to the lamb, "I deserve what I get, for I'm a wolf and it isn't my job to be a piper!"

"Hah-hah!" laughed the lamb, and kept dancing to mock the fleeing wolf. But as he danced, his mother and the other sheep disappeared over a hill, and the lamb, left alone, very soon starved to death.

If you happen to be a lamb, it's not your job to be a dancer.

Hermes and the blind seer

Hermes decided to test the magical powers of Tiresias, the blind seer of Thebes. He disguised himself as a human, stole the seer's cattle, and hid them under a hill.

Then he approached Tiresias and told him that his cattle were gone. "Can you find them by divination of the birds?" Hermes challenged the seer.

"Take me to the country," the blind seer said, "and we'll find a flock of ravens."

Soon Hermes led Tiresias to some ravens quietly twittering on the limb of an oak tree.

"Are the birds that I hear ravens?" Tiresias asked Hermes.

"Yes," Hermes replied.

Then Tiresias said to the birds, "*Well?*"

And the ravens began to caw loudly.

"What do they say?" Hermes asked.

"They say that you may return my cattle any time you wish," said the prophet.

If you're going to steal cattle from a blind seer, don't let the ravens see what you're up to.

Hermes and the cloak of lies

Zeus asked Hermes to make a cloak of lies for every poet and artisan he could find. And Hermes made the cloaks, and draped them on artisans everywhere, but he couldn't find a poet. Finally, after many days of searching, he discovered one reciting his verses to a rapt crowd in the agora of a town, and he fashioned a cloak of lies of triple cloth for the poet. The poet recited three times the verses he had intended to, and in the end the crowd crowned him with laurel.

[See the moral to the fable "The man, the lion, and the statue," above.]

Hermes and the Arabs

Zeus sent the devious Hermes to spread as many lies on earth as he could. Hermes drove his chariot from country to country, performing his mission well. But when he came to the land of the Arabs, the wheels came off his chariot, and the Arabs stole its contents, and so they acquired more than their share of lies.

Thus it is that the Arabs lie more than any other people. Indeed, there's no word for "truth" in their language!

. . . So ends the original fable. But if there's no word for "truth" in the language of a people, how can there be a word for "lie"?

The eunuch and the shaman

A kindly eunuch sent a scroll to a shaman asking him to offer up a sacrifice on his behalf, so that he might be a father. But when the shaman saw the eunuch in person, he mocked him, saying, "I asked the gods to make you a father, but on meeting you I see that you aren't even a man!"

Just then a lion leaped from behind a tree, caught the shaman, and made to devour him. The kindly eunuch, who couldn't bear to see harm come to another, asked the lion to devour him instead. Thus the shaman was spared.

A eunuch is a eunuch, but there's more than one way to be a man.

The adder, the water-snake, and the frogs

An adder and a water-snake argued about who was entitled to drink from a pool in the forest. Each claimed the pool as his territory, and since they couldn't resolve their dispute, they decided to do battle. The frogs, who had no fondness for the water-snake, told the adder that they were on his side. The two snakes struggled and struggled, but all the frogs could do was to look on and croak mightily for the adder to win.

Finally the adder prevailed, but he criticized the frogs for doing nothing to help except croak.

"But, friend," the frogs replied. "That's what we were born to do!"

"In that case," acknowledged the adder, "I'm grateful to you, little friends."

Cheerleaders have their place in the grand scheme of things, but only in competitions between adders and water-snakes.

Zeus, the fox, and the cockchafer

Once upon a time Zeus noted how clever the fox was, and decided to make him king of all the animals. But the god wanted to know, in changing from a commoner to a king, whether the fox had also changed his old habit of covetousness, which isn't becoming of royalty. Zeus sent a cockchafer[3] to tempt the fox (who hadn't changed his habit of covetousness one bit), but since the fox hadn't the foggiest notion what a cockchafer was, he chose to let it alone, and Zeus allowed the fox to remain king of the animals!

Royalty may be skin deep, but ignorance is bliss, even for clever foxes.

---

3. A cockchafer is a species of beetle.

Zeus and Hermes

Zeus decided to send Hermes to earth to pour intelligence over men. But the mischievous Hermes had ideas of his own. He poured intelligence only over tall, handsome men and short, ugly men, knowing full well that the latter would therefore have more sense and the former less.

Down to earth *beats* head in the clouds, *but women still go for tall, dark, and handsome.*

Zeus and Apollo

Zeus and Apollo held an archery match. Apollo went first, picked up his bow, and shot an arrow fast and far. Then Zeus, to put Apollo in his place, took three giant strides, outdistancing Apollo's mighty shot; but in doing so he received Apollo's arrow in his naked buttocks!

By competing with rivals weaker than we are, whom we can easily overtake, we expose ourselves to ridicule.

Zeus and the jar of good things

Zeus decided to put good things in a large wine jar, and gave it to a man for safekeeping. But the man, curious to know what was inside, opened the lid, and the good things flew all the way back up to Olympus. The gods, who already had more good things than they needed, gave them to charity.

Better to give than to receive, but only if you live on Olympus.

Zeus, Prometheus, Athena, and the minor god Momos

Zeus made a man, Prometheus made a bull, and Athena made a house. They asked the minor god Momos to judge the worth of their work, but Momos, being a jealous god, had little good to say. He criticized Zeus, saying that he should have put man's mind outside his body, so that his shortcomings would be visible to all; he criticized Prometheus for not putting the bull's eyes on his horns, so he could better see what he was attacking; and he criticized Athena for not putting wheels on the house, so that its inhabitants could roll it away if they lived next to bad neighbors.

Enraged, Zeus, Prometheus, and Athena banished Momos forever.

Everybody's a critic, even on Olympus.

Zeus and the tortoise

The animals were invited to Zeus's wedding on heavenly Olympus, but a poor tortoise failed to show. When Zeus later asked him why, the tortoise said, "My humble home is dear, my home is best."

"In that case," said Zeus, enraged. "I condemn you to carry your humble home everywhere on your back!"

"But have mercy on me!" pleaded the poor tortoise.

"Very well," Zeus replied. "I won't charge you rent."

Thank heavenly Olympus for small favors.

The mule and the race

A mule was feeling full of pride and thought,

"My father is a fast-running horse, and I take after him!" The mule entered a race, but at the last minute the father decided to enter too, and won the race.

"Oh, well," the mule acknowledged, "I was merely lying to myself, for my father is really an ass."

Don't depend on your father to fight your battles, lest you make an ass of yourself.

The bird-catcher and the asp

A bird-catcher laid his traps, walking from tree to tree, climbing each one, and carefully placing his snares and oak-gum. But when he descended the last tree, he grew careless and stepped on an asp, which bit him.

Knowing the asp's bite was fatal, the bird-catcher lamented, "Surely this was meant to be. I, a wicked man that captured harmless creatures of the air in my snares, was ensnared by a wicked creature of the earth!"

Then Death appeared and said to him,

"Wrong, my friend! This was a stroke of bad fortune, nothing more and nothing less. Besides," he added, "now your wearisome tree-climbing days are over and your worldly cares are done with!"

"You know, I never looked at it that way," acknowledged the bird-catcher, and died.

Better to be unlucky than good.

The sick man and the quack

A man fell ill and sent for a doctor, who happened to be a quack. After taking his money, the quack gave him some medicines and quickly departed. Shortly thereafter a neighbor called and told the sick man the truth about the doctor, and that it was very unwise to take any medicines he'd prescribed. Thus the man threw the medicines away, and, as it happened, returned to health on his own.

A few days later he ventured out, and ran into the quack doctor in the agora. The quack, thinking that the man must have died and that he was talking to a ghost, said,

"Well, my unfortunate friend, how are things down below?"

The man thought to play a joke on the quack.

"I gave them your name," he said. "They assured me they'd send you the same pestilence that afflicted me!"

And the quack ran into the street, shouting, "Oh, help! Help! What am I to do?"

Even quack physicians ought to heal themselves.

The sick man and the doctor

A man lay ill. His friends argued among themselves about what to do, each one scolding the man for not taking his particular advice. Finally the man cried out, "You weary me to distraction with all this arguing and scolding. Please summon a doctor!"

The doctor was summoned, shooed the quarrelsome friends from the sickroom, and examined the man.

"What do you prescribe for me?" asked the man.

"The only thing that can save you," the doctor said, "is treatment with wooden enemas."

The man refused, and he died shortly thereafter.

After the man was buried, the doctor told the friends,

"He would've lived if he'd taken treatments with wooden enemas, as I prescribed."

Then the friends scolded the doctor,

"But if you'd told him that when he was alive, he wouldn't have died!"

"I did tell him!" the doctor protested. "He said he'd rather die than take the enemas I prescribed."

. . . With enemas like those, who needs friends?

The kite and the serpent

There was a pious serpent that enjoyed passing judgment on his fellow creatures. One day a kite swooped down, picked him up in its claws, and flew away! But the serpent struggled and struggled, and the two fell to earth. The unfortunate kite was killed outright, and its ghost flew off to the Underworld.

"You see?" the mortally-injured serpent loudly hissed after him. "This is what happens when you attempt to wrong some-one who's done you no harm! I was simply slithering along, minding my own business, when . . ." And he continued to pontificate and scold the fleeing ghost of the kite that couldn't wait to reach the Underworld, well out of hearing of the serpent's pious judgments.

If a serpent is so bold as to pass judgment on you, tell him to go fly a kite.

The horse and the mill-wheel

An old horse was sold to a man who hitched it to a mill-wheel. As the horse began his work he groaned and lamented,

"First it was the wearisome turn of the race-track, now I am condemned to the wearisome turn of this mill-wheel! Oh, woe is me!"

One bad turn deserves another.

The groom and the horse

A groom decided to sell half the barley he was supposed to feed the horse in his charge.

"But that isn't right!" protested the horse.

"Well," said the groom, "here's what I'll do. To make up for half the barley, I'll spend all day in the stable grooming and currying you, and you'll boast the shiniest coat in the countryside!"

In time the poor horse died of having too little to eat. When he was lowered into the earth, the other animals all marveled that he was the best-groomed and -curried horse they'd ever seen!

Every silver lining has a dark cloud.

The reed and the olive tree

A reed and an olive tree were in dispute concerning their strength. As the olive kept boasting that he was much larger and stronger, the reed fell silent and kept his own counsel. Then a very strong wind came up and broke the olive tree in half, while the supple reed bent easily back and forth and was spared. The shattered olive tree said, "Wait and see, my friend! There are olives everywhere now, and each one will produce another tree just like me!"

There's more than one way to blow with the wind.

The ape and the piglet

The camel and the elephant argued about who should rule over all the animals. But the ape came between them, saying,

"How could either of you be king? Look here!" and he set a piglet down before them, and, frightened by such a small, wiggly thing, the camel and the elephant ran off!

"You see?" said the ape to the other animals, "how could *they* have defended us from our enemies? I, who have both size and strength to spare, should be king!"

But the other animals, very impressed by what they had seen, named the piglet their king instead.

An ape may have size to spare, but a piglet is every inch a king.

The camel-driver and the sitting camel

A camel-driver ordered his camel to dance. As the camel danced, the camel-driver laughed. But the camel said,

"Not only do you laugh at me when I dance, you laugh at me when I walk!" Then the camel sat down on his haunches and refused to move; but the camel-driver laughed even harder.

You won't get much work out of a sitting camel, but you might get a few laughs.

Zeus and the camel

A camel, envying the bull its mighty horns, asked Zeus to give him horns as well. But Zeus, angry that the camel wasn't satisfied with his own strength and size alone, put a ridiculous-looking hump on his back as punishment. And the camel said,

"Woe is me! Now I must walk through the desert with this good-for-nothing hump!"

Even a camel ought to know that there's a lid for every pot.

The two scarab beetles

Two scarab beetles lived on an island with a herd of cattle. The beetles made a good enough living eating dung, but on a fall day one beetle said to the other,

"I believe I'll fly over to the mainland to see if the food they have there is better than here. If the food *is* better, I'll spend the winter and bring you back some in the spring." And he flew away to the mainland, where he indeed found better kinds of dung; and he ate his fill all winter.

When he returned to the island in the spring, his friend saw that he was more fat and healthy-looking than ever, but chided him for not bringing any of the better delicacies to him, as he'd promised. "Yes," said the other, "there was plenty to live on over there, but you can't bring it back with you after all!"

1. Better to live on dung than on expectations.
2. Grass fertilized with dung is always greener.

The crab and the fox

A crab decided to leave the sea and begin a new life on shore. A hungry fox, spotting it crawling about on the sand, pounced and caught the unfortunate creature in its paws.

"Fool!" chided the fox, putting on his dinner bib. "You left your comfortable home there in the sea to come to the shore where danger awaited you! Do you see us foxes leaving our comfortable home on the shore to go live in the sea?"

And the fox devoured the crab, shell and all.

Nothing protects a crustacean from outfoxing itself.

The mother crab and her offspring

A mother crab said to her offspring,

"Don't walk sideways, children! Walk straight!"

"Oh?" said the little crabs. "Let's see you walk straight! Then we'll copy you!"

The mother spanked the children for their insolence and insubordination.

Being a crab is no excuse for sassing your mother.

The thieves and the cockerel that did things by the numbers

Once there was a cockerel that was known for his precision in counting down to the right hour, minute, and second of day-break to crow. But one day he was stolen by thieves, who made to boil him for dinner, when he said,

"One, two, three,
Please don't sacrifice me!"

"Why, this bird can count!" said the thieves, astonished.

"Yes," said the cockerel, "and I'm so skilled at counting down to the exact second of daybreak that you can be up and about thieving right on time!"

"That's a good point!" agreed the thieves. "Well, we'll spare you if you promise to join us."

And the cockerel said,

"One, two, three,
A thief I shall be!"

And the cockerel and the thieves lived happily ever after.

Cockerels subtract from sleep, but add to honor among thieves.

The stomach and the feet

The stomach and the feet were arguing about which was stronger and more useful. The feet claimed they were superior because they carried the stomach from place to place.

"Ah," said the stomach, "but it's I that nourish you so that you may have the strength to carry me!"

"Very well," said the feet. "We'll stop walking and *then* see where you get your nourishment, my friend."

"Fools!" rejoined the stomach. "If you do such a thing, you too will suffer and we'll both die!"

"Why, that's true!" the feet agreed. "We never thought of it that way."

In a dispute between the stomach and the feet—and, come to think of it, in every contention involving superiority of parts of the body—put your money on the stomach.

The lion, the fox, and the monkey

An elderly lion enjoyed hosting lavish feasts in his den. He invited so many of the beasts of the wild that the den became crowded; the guest-list included bucks and does, foxes and bears, frogs and snakes, asses and horses, cows and oxen. His companion, a fox, shared in the festivities, while an elderly monkey cooked and served the food.

One day the lion noticed that the fox was disconsolate, and he asked why.

"It's only that, when you invite someone new, all I get is leftovers from the previous feast, and I'm afraid that soon *I* shall have nothing to eat."

Then the lion chortled so loud and so long, rolling over and over on the floor of the den, that the fox was astounded that he should make such a fool of himself.

"Oh, don't blame me, little one," said the lion when he recovered himself. "It's the monkey who cooks and serves for all of our friends!"

When a lion makes an ass of himself in passing the buck to a monkey, it's time to get a bigger den.

The abbots and the monks

A monk gave his abbots three meals a day, but they were dissatisfied and prayed to Zeus to take this abbot and send them another one. But when the first abbot died, his replacement gave them two meals a day, so that again they prayed to Zeus, who sent a third abbot; but this one gave them just one meal. Then one abbot said to the others,

"We'd better pray to Zeus to let us keep this abbot, or we'll surely starve!"

If you want to work up a good appetite, take one step forward, two steps back.

The fox and the jackdaw

A hungry jackdaw sat in a fig tree waiting for the figs to ripen.
A fox happened by and said, "My friend, give up your vigil;
you're living off hope, and hope, as they say, is an illusion!"

"You're right, my friend," and the hungry jackdaw flew off.
But soon the figs ripened, and the clever fox ate them all.

*Patient foxes win the day; jackdaws that don't care a fig for
illusions go hungry anyway.*

The very large jackdaw

A jackdaw grew much larger than the other jackdaws, and so refused to associate with them. He went to the ravens, and asked if he could join them, but the ravens, puzzled by the jackdaw's different looks and different voice, chased him away. Then the jackdaw, realizing his mistake, returned to his own kind; but they, angry that he'd shunned them, refused him. Thus the unfortunate jackdaw had nowhere to go.

If you've screwed up your life in one corner of the world, you've screwed it up everywhere.

The jackdaw and the birds

Zeus decided to name an emperor of the birds. He gathered them and said,

"Go prepare yourselves, my little friends, for the most beautiful bird shall be your emperor!" Then Zeus went back to Olympus, and the excited birds went down to the river to wash up.

Now the jackdaw knew full well that he was the ugliest of birds and therefore had no chance to win the contest; so he sneaked after the others and stole the feathers that had fallen off during the washing. Then he placed them over his own nondescript feathers.

When Zeus returned to judge the birds, the jackdaw caught his eye immediately. "Lo!" said Zeus, "this is the most beautiful of birds! *He* shall be your emperor!"

But the other birds, angry at the jackdaw, pecked at him until they reclaimed their own feathers, and the jackdaw was revealed for what he was, and was emperor no more.

Whether he pretends to have clothes or feathers, a naked emperor is a naked emperor.

The jackdaw that escaped slavery

A man trapped a jackdaw, attached a long string to its claws, and gave it to his child. But the jackdaw pecked through the string, escaped, and flew back to the forest. Alas, the string which still dangled from its claws became hopelessly tangled in a branch, and the jackdaw was trapped forever.

"Woe is me!" said the jackdaw. "Because I did not wish to be a slave, I've now sacrificed my life!"

Better a live slave than a dead jackdaw.

The raven, the dog, and Athena

A prophetic raven decided to make a hecatomb in honor of Athena, which, in the case of birds, is the sacrifice of a hundred mice. As the raven made preparations, a dog happened by and said,

"Why do you waste your time in this fashion? Athena could care less about mice, and besides, I have it on good authority that she despises you, and is about to discredit all your signs and portents."

"But that's precisely why I offer up sacrifice," the raven insisted. "I know she despises me, but with the hecatomb I hope to win back her favors!"

And it came to pass that Athena, once the raven had made the hecatomb, smiled on him and gave him many new signs and portents.

Flattery gets you nowhere, but appeasement wins the day.

The ploughman's child and the snails

A ploughman's child was baking some snails. As they began to sputter and hop about, she said,

"Why, what foolish creatures you are! Your homes are on fire and yet you sing and dance."

"Oh," said the snails cheerfully. "These are but temporary dwellings. We spend the rest of our time in our homes deep in the forest!"

In saying this they roasted, and the child ate them, shells and all.

Home is where the heart is, but the brains, that's a different matter.

The farmer and the swan

A farmer owned a goose and a swan. He kept the swan for its voice and the goose for eating purposes. When it came time to kill the goose, the farmer went to the barnyard, but as it was getting dark, he picked up the swan instead and prepared to wring its neck. Frightened, the swan began to sing, and the farmer, recognizing its voice, turned his attentions to the goose.

The next day a runaway ox-cart entered the barnyard and crushed the neck of the swan.

No swan song cheats death for long.

The raven and the gods

A very sick raven told its mother,

"Don't cry, mother, instead, beseech the gods to send a sign that they'll cure me of my illness."

But the mother raven said, "How can the gods look kindly on you, my dear son, for you steal their food!"

"But I haven't stolen their ambrosia, mother," said the sick raven. "I've only stolen the offerings left on altars and in temples!"

The gods refused to send a sign to the sick raven, and he croaked in due time.

Gods don't split hairs.

The two crested larks [a Creation Myth]

In the beginning there was a crested lark and his daughter, who were created before anything else. When the father died, the daughter had no place to lay him to rest, because the earth did not yet exist; and so she buried him in the many feathers of her crest, and honored him in that fashion.

Before the creation of the heavens and the earth, a crested lark carried around the dead body of her father on her head. Go figure.

The raven and the chough

A raven and a chough were friends and flew everywhere to-gether. The chough envied the raven his ability to foretell things to come, and asked him for instruction.

"Gladly," the raven said, and gave the chough some valuable advice.

Soon two poor and weary vagabonds happened by. The raven and the chough circled overhead, and the raven said to his friend, "Very well, here's a chance to try out your new powers!" And the chough began squawking of signs and portents.

One vagabond looked up. "See there," he said to his companion, "a bird of prophecy!"

"Oh, hell, what do we care?" shrugged the other. "Things are dreadful enough for us in the here and now. Do you really want to know what they'll be like in the future?"

They passed on.

Birds of a feather flock together, but if nobody cares a fig about signs and portents, what does that matter?

The two dogs

A hunter owned two dogs. One dog he kept at home as a guard and the other he took with him hunting in the woods. When they returned with fresh meat which the hunting dog had caught, its owner gave it to the guard dog: whereupon the hunting dog said to his brother, "Damn it, that isn't fair. I do all the work and you get the reward, even though you stay home and sleep all day!"

"It's not my fault," said the guard dog, gnawing on the bone of a stag that the other had killed. "It's our owner's fault, for he ordered me to do this."

Zeus overheard these irresponsible words and, angered, sent a thunderbolt which killed the guard dog.

Don't pass the buck
And tempt your luck.

The two starving dogs

Two starving dogs spotted some hides a farmer had left to soften in the river. Seeing that the hides were too far to reach, the dogs drank as much water as they could in order to get to them. They drank and drank, until, alas, both of them burst!

A passing vagabond who saw what happened said, "Ah, well, it's all the same. These poor starving dogs would've choked to death on the hides anyway!"

. . . *It still pays to eliminate the middleman.*

The man, the dog, and the townspeople

A man was bitten on the leg by a dog. He searched in the town for someone to heal his wound. The townspeople said, "Wipe the wound with bread and throw it to the dog that bit you; then your leg will heal."

"Alas," replied the man, "if I do that, every dog in town will be after me!"

Always count on paying for free advice.

The woodchopper and the trees

One cold autumn day a woodchopper asked the trees which one of them had the hardest wood for his axe handles. The trees conferred, finally choosing the olive. But once the wood-chopper had made his handles, he proceeded to chop *all* the trees down, beginning with the olive, and he and his family kept warm for the winter.

Show me a tree that can't get a handle on the situation, and I'll show you a tree that can't handle the fireplace.

The dog that ran away

A dog was trained to do battle with the beasts of the forest. One day, seeing a bear and a wolf brought into the arena, he ran off into the town. Some other dogs asked him why he had run away, and he said,

"It's true that I'm very well fed, but fighting bears and wolves is risky business!" The other dogs said to each other, "Oh, ho, but *we* are well taken care of, and *we* don't have to fight bears and wolves!"

[See moral to "The two starving dogs," above.]

The cranes, the stork, and the farmer's seeds

A family of cranes was in the habit of harassing a farmer by eating all the seeds he sowed in his fields. A stork happened to make his home with the cranes, but he, being an honest bird, refused to participate in the thefts of the farmer's seeds.

Finally the farmer, tired of losing his seeds, set a snare, catching the cranes and the stork together, killing them all, guilty and innocent alike.

You can't always tell a stork by the company he keeps.

The cockerel, the dog, and the fox

A dog and a cockerel became friends, and walked down a country road. As night approached, the cockerel perched on the branch, and the dog went to sleep in the hollow of an oak tree.

Soon a fox appeared and said to the cockerel, "Please come down, friend, because I wish to throw my arms around someone with such a beautiful voice as yours."

"I *will* come down," the cockerel nodded, "if you'll awaken the doorkeeper asleep in the hollow of this tree."

The fox duly awakened the dog. The dog, in turn, promptly killed him.

[Original moral]: If they are able, men of common sense pass their enemies on to those who are better equipped to defend them.

Our moral: If you can't let sleeping dogs lie, at least stop chasing after cockerels.

The hound and the hare

In a summer fallow field, a hound seized a hare, trying to bite it and lick his chops, all at the same time! Finally the hare said,

"Fool, either bite me or kiss me, so that I may know whether you are enemy or friend." And the hound bit him.

Wise in the ways of the world, the hare said, "Hah! Some friend!" adding, "I would've expected an enemy to kiss me!"

Cultivate your enemies; at least you know where you stand.

The dog and the bell

A dog was in the habit of biting people, so his owner placed a bell around his neck to warn villagers of his approach. Proud of the bell, the dog went down to the agora and walked up and down, shaking it with great vigor. But another dog heard the bell and said,

"What are you so proud of? The bell has nothing to do with your good, but with your bad qualities."

"That makes little difference to me," sniffed the dog with the bell, and bit the other on the haunch!

No matter for whom or what it tolls, a bell is a bell.

The lion and the hunting dog with sensitive hearing

A hunting dog pursued a lion. But when the lion let out a terrible roar, the dog ran away. Whereupon another dog said to him,

"You make as if to hunt the king of beasts, and you can't even abide their roar!"

"No, no; it's not that I'm afraid," protested the hunting dog. "You see, I have very sensitive hearing, and the roaring of the lion causes me great pain!"

Now the lion, overhearing his, ceased his roaring, slowly and silently crept up through the foliage, and devoured the hunting dog with sensitive hearing.

Better to get an earful than to be a bellyful.

The hares and the foxes

Once there was a war between the hares and the eagles. The hares asked the foxes to join them, but the foxes said, "We respectfully decline, for we know who you are and with whom you are fighting!"

[Original moral] Those foolish enough to fight their superiors have no respect for the rules of safety.

Our moral: If you must take sides in a dispute, always choose the adversary with sharp claws.

The hares and the frogs

The hares gathered to bemoan their fate. Prey to lions, eagles, serpents, and foxes, they believed that their lives were so miserable that they decided to do away with themselves.

Thus they rushed down to a pond to drown their sorrows, but the frogs, hearing the approach of the hares, became frightened, and leaped into the water before them. And one hare said, "Friends, hold on! Don't jump in the pond! Instead, look at these creatures that are even more fearful of living than we are!"

There's more than one way to have your cake and gag on it too.

The lion and the eagle

A lion and an eagle decided to become friends. But the lion said,

"You must give me your wing feathers as a pledge of friendship." The eagle agreed, then said to the lion, "And you must give me your mane as a pledge of friendship." The lion, too, agreed, donning the eagle's feathers, whereupon the eagle donned the lion's mane.

Question: What's the most ridiculous damn thing imaginable?
Answer: Friendship between a lion and an eagle.

The gnat, the lion, and the spider

A gnat said to a lion, "You're much bigger than I am, but I'll wager I can outfight you!"

"Done!" said the lion, and he prepared for battle. But the gnat flew into the lion's nose and began biting and biting him, until the lion clawed at himself frantically, causing much pain and loss of blood. Finally the poor lion ran away.

Then the gnat, puffed up with pride, flew around the forest, bragging of his prowess. But he grew careless and landed in a spider's web. As he was about to be devoured, the gnat lamented, "Woe is me, that I, the new king of beasts, should have been brought to such a pass by an ordinary spider."

It takes two to weave a web of deception.

The seagull and the kite

A seagull swallowed a fish for dinner, but the fish got caught in its gullet. The unfortunate gull died, and its ghost flew to the Underworld. Then a kite happened by, saw the seagull's body lying on the beach, and said,

"Serves you right, my friend! You were a bird, and you should've earned your living on land, not in the sea!"

Just then a succulent young crab came out of the sea onto the land, and the kite, unable to resist, devoured it. His gullet, too, burst, and the ghost followed the seagull's ghost down to the Underworld.

There the seagull and the kite bickered for all eternity about who got what he deserved, and why.

. . . Next time someone tells you that the world is governed by poetic justice, don't quarrel; just let it go, even as the seagull and the kite should've let go of their catches.

The vixen and the lioness

A vixen haughtily criticized a lioness for having only one child.

"It's true that I have just one," replied the lioness equally haughtily, "but he's a lion nonetheless!"

Take quality over quantity, except in the case of only children, who, like as not, are spoiled rotten.

The lion and the fox

An old, sick lion had to resort to trickery to obtain his food. Remaining in his cave, he promised the animals a hearty dinner if they would enter. When they entered, he kept his promise by eating them for dinner! But, lions being what they are, he was never satisfied.

Then a fox happened by, but hesitated. The lion said, "Why not come in for dinner, my friend?"

The fox said, "I'd do so, except that I see that the footprints of my brethren lead in to your cave, but none lead out!"

The lion thought a moment; then he said,

"But would you enter if the footprints led out of the cave as well?"

"No, no, that wouldn't at all be satisfactory!" exclaimed the fox. "For clearly it would mean that your company is not worth keeping!"

Avoid the company of those who never get enough.

The ploughman and the lion

A ploughman left his barn door open and a lion sneaked in. He commenced to dine on the sheep, oxen, and cattle that lived in the barn.

The ploughman's wife was beside herself and shouted at her husband,

"This is a fine state of affairs! What do you plan to do with the lion once he's eaten all of our livestock?"

"No, my dear," said the ploughman. "The question is, what does the lion plan to do with us?"

The essence of folly is to plan ahead too late.

The lion and the dull-witted ploughman's daughter

A lion fell in love with the daughter of a dull-witted ploughman, and asked for her hand in marriage. Afraid of the prospect of having such a ferocious son-in-law, the ploughman told the lion he'd grant his request if the beast would have his teeth and claws removed. The lion agreed, but once the operation was performed, the ploughman told him to get the hell back where he came from.

"But why do you send me away?" asked the lion.

"It just occurred to me," answered the ploughman. "What on earth would the children of a marriage between a lion and a girl look like?"

It's OK to be slow on the uptake, providing that the lion has no claws or teeth.

The lion, the bear, and the fox

A bear and a lion fought over the carcass of a fawn in the forest. They exchanged many blows to the head and face, until finally both of them collapsed. A fox happened by, saw the fawn and the two fighters lying on their backs, and took the fawn, saving it for a tasty supper.

The bear said to the lion, "Woe is us, to have gone through all of this just to feed a fox!"

Then the lion said to the bear, "But this has given me new strength! Let's go after the fox."

And, reinvigorated, the bear and the lion chased after the fox, caught him, and enjoyed the fox for supper and the fawn for dessert.

It's deadly easy to outfox a punch-drunk bear and a punch-drunk lion.

The lion, the fox, and the stag

A sick and aging lion asked the fox, his neighbor, to induce a stag to come to his cave, for he could no longer hunt with ease.

"I've wanted to devour a stag for a long time," said the lion. "Especially the heart!"

And so the fox went into the forest, found a stag drinking at a pool, and told him that the lion lay ill and dying and wished to anoint the stag the new king of animals. The stag, puffed up with pride, agreed to accompany the fox back to the lion's cave, whereupon the lion managed to seize him and eat his entrails and bones, even the marrow; but the heart fell to the floor of the cave. The fox, seeing the heart, devoured it himself, thinking it just compensation for the errand he had run for the lion.

The lion, still hungry, asked the fox what happened to the heart.

"The stag had no heart, your majesty," said the fox in a trembling voice. "How could an animal be said to have a heart that was foolish enough to enter a lion's den under such a flimsy pretext?"

"You're talking about the brains, you fool, not the heart!" said the lion, and devoured the fox in one piece.

Show me a fox that flunks Anatomy 101 and I'll show you a fox with no anatomy, period.

The frog, the lion, and Zeus

A lion heard a frog croaking loudly in the woods. Thinking that the frog was as large as he, the lion approached the pond where the frog lived, but, seeing that he was so small, caught him and crushed him.

"Such loud noises from one so very small!" the lion roared.

Then Zeus, seeing what had happened, strode across the mountains and crushed the lion.

"Such loud noises from one so very small!" said the King of the Gods.

Frogs and lions would do better to keep their own counsel.

The lion and the wild boar

A lion and a wild boar went down to a spring to drink. But since there wasn't enough water for both of them, they decided to have a contest of strength to see which one could vanquish the other and have the spring to himself. The competition began, and they struggled and struggled, but soon they stopped, noticing that vultures had gathered nearby to see who would win. Then the lion said to the boar,

"This is silly. Better we become friends than food for vultures!"

It matters not whether you win or lose, but how you play the game.

The lion and the dolphin

A lion traveled to the seashore. He told a passing dolphin, "You and I should be friends, for I'm king of beasts on the land and you're king of beasts in the sea!"

"Very well, my friend," agreed the dolphin.

Time passed, and the lion returned to the shore.

"Friend, I need your help," he said to the dolphin, "for a wild bull has picked me for his enemy."

"Friend, I cannot walk on the land," said the dolphin. "Besides, a whale has picked me for *its* enemy."

"Bah!" said the lion. "Let me demonstrate to you that we *can* help one another." And, intent on pursuing the whale, he leaped in the waves, and drowned.

Better to know your friends than to be picked by your enemies.

The lion, the fox, and the ass

A lion, a fox, and an ass made a pact to divide the spoils of a hunting expedition. When they'd chased down an abundance of deer, rabbits, and other game, the lion told the ass to divide the game. The ass divided it all into three equal portions, whereupon the lion grew angry and devoured him. Then the lion asked the fox to divide the game. The fox portioned out a very large lion's share, leaving only a morsel or two, which he gobbled up.

"Good work, my friend!" said the delighted lion, sitting down to his meal. "But aren't you being unfair to yourself?"

Not wanting to remind the lion of what happened to the ass, the fox carefully replied, "No, your majesty. It's simply that I have a small appetite."

It's one thing to learn from another's bad luck; quite another to flout it.

The lion and the elephant

A lion confided in an elephant that he, the king of beasts, was ashamed because he was frightened of cockerels. Just then a gnat flew onto the head of the elephant. The elephant's ears began to flap and twitch, and he said, "Oh, sweet Prometheus! A gnat! That tiny creature will get in my ears and will be the end of me!" And the great creature turned and lumbered into the jungle.

"I'll be damned," thought the lion, "I don't feel so ashamed after all!"

[Original moral]: One sees that the gnat is strong enough to make even an elephant fearful.

Our moral: Everything is relative, even in the jungle.

The lion and the bull

A lion invited a bull to supper. The bull, seeing that the spits and cauldrons were about his own size, asked the lion why.

"Oh," the lion assured him, "Those are for the goats and sheep that happen by, and which will furnish our supper."

"I may be a bull, my friend," said the bull, "but I'm not as foolish as you suppose."

"But aren't you hungry?"

"Yes," the bull said, "but I see no goats and sheep. In any case, the real question is, aren't you hungry, my friend?" And he ran off before the lion could reply.

Keep your spits and cauldrons out of plain view, or everybody goes hungry.

The stag and the lion

An enraged lion roared and roared. A stag, hearing the roars, said, "Sweet Prometheus, woe is us! This lion is dangerous enough when he's calm; and just listen to him now!"

As well be devoured by an enraged lion as by a calm one.

The lion, the mouse, and the fox

Once there was a lion that was afraid of mice. When he was sleeping, a mouse jumped on his back and ran up and down; the lion, waking with a start, rolled over and over again, roaring in fear. A fox happened by and said, "Look at you, the king of beasts, afraid of a little mouse!"

"Oh, no," the lion protested. "I was simply surprised that such a small creature could be so foolish as to leap onto the back of a sleeping lion!"

"I'm not quite sure that I believe you, my friend," said the fox.

"It's not important that you believe me," replied the lion. "It's only important that I believe me."

[Original moral]: Wise men keep an eye on the little things.

Our moral: It's easier to fool yourself all of the time than to fool a fox some of the time.

The bandit and the mulberry tree

A bandit killed a man on the road. After he hid the body in a culvert, a group of men happened by.

"What are those red stains on your hands, my friend?" one inquired.

"Oh," said the bandit in a trembling voice, "I just climbed a mulberry tree!"

Suspicious, another man looked in the culvert and found the body of the bandit's victim.

"If you're so fond of mulberry trees, my friend," he said, "we'll be more than happy to oblige you."

Then, as they were hanging the bandit from the nearest mulberry tree, the miscreant cried out for help.

"Don't look at me, my friend!" said the tree. "I'm not the one with blood on my hands!"

Few wish to take responsibility in this world; whether they should do so is a different matter.

The dogs and the Athenian general

The dogs and the wolves prepared for war. The dogs asked an Athenian general to lead them, but the general said,

"Take heed, my friends; the wolves are all the same breed, all the same color. You, on the other hand, are of many colors and many breeds. Just look at you! Maltese terriers, Spartan hounds, Corinthian mastiffs, Thracian . . ." The general enumerated breed after breed after breed, talking until the sun went down in the sky. In the end, he said,

"Besides, my friends, the wolves are bigger and have more stamina than you; surely they'll tear you to pieces!"

The dogs, utterly worn out by the general's words, said,

"Why didn't you tell us that in the first place?"

Avoid war by any means possible.

The wolves and the ram

The wolves told the sheep that they would make peace with them if they would only give up their dogs. The leader of the sheep, a ram, said,

"Why should we do that when, even when we're guarded by the dogs, it's impossible to graze in safety?"

"But if it's impossible to graze in safety with the dogs," said the wolves to the ram, "what difference does it make if you're without them?"

"Why, I never thought of it that way!" said the ram.

Then he advised the sheep to give up the dogs. The wolves, of course, promptly devoured the sheep, starting with the ram.

Even a ram should know that logic has its limitations.

The wolf proud of his shadow

A wolf was trotting down a country road. It was late in the day, and he noticed how large and intimidating the setting sun made his shadow.

"Now just look at that!" the wolf said, puffed up with pride. "Surely I, not the lion, should be king of beasts!"

Just then a lion, overhearing the wolf's proud words, leaped out from behind a bush and devoured him!

Then, a muffled voice:

"You may digest me, my friend, but you can't digest my shadow!"

Always look on the sunny side.

The silly wolf and the lamb

A hungry wolf spotted a lamb drinking at a stream and sought a good reason for devouring it.

"Look at you," he said. "You're muddying the waters that *I* drink from."

"No, you silly wolf," argued the lamb. "I'm downstream from you. And," he added, "I only use the tip of my tongue when I drink."

"Well, then," said the wolf after thinking this over, "You made fun of my father last year!"

"I wasn't born last year, you imbecile," said the lamb.

"Well, then," the wolf went on, "You . . ." and he kept justifying as the lamb kept drinking. Finally, out of breath, he said, "Never mind! I'll eat you all the same!"

"Then why," asked the lamb, "did you waste time resorting to all those stupid arguments?"

". . . Why, I never thought of it that way," the wolf replied. "You've taught me something today, my friend. In exchange, I won't eat you after all!"

Nothing whets the appetite like a good argument, but don't tell it to a wolf.

The argumentative wolf and the argumentative heron

At the edge of a pond a wolf caught a fish and ate it, but a large bone got stuck in its throat. A heron happened by and the wolf croaked,

"Please help me, my friend!"

When the wolf promised to pay him, the heron put his head in the wolf's throat and retrieved the bone.

"Well," said the heron, "where's my fee?"

"Ah! You just stuck your head down a wolf's throat with no bad consequences for you," said the wolf. "That should be fee enough!"

"But if you hadn't been in distress, my head wouldn't have been in your throat in the first place!" insisted the heron.

"But . . ."

"But . . ."

The two continued to dispute the matter all day and all night until the other animals in the forest begged for peace and quiet!

After a reasonable point, all disputants gag on the bone of contention.

The wolf-king and the ass

The king of the wolves proposed that all should share their catches equally so that everyone would have enough to eat. The wolves agreed to this proposition, but just then an ass happened by and said to the king in a haughty manner,

"That's well and good for you, your majesty, but what about the deer that you caught this morning and hid in your cave? That should be a lesson to you! And furthermore . . ."

"OK, OK, I'm well rebuked," interrupted the wolf-king, and shared the deer with the others. But as the others were busy devouring the deer, the wolf-king killed the ass, dragged him into his cave, and ate his fill.

If you must pontificate, do so at a distance.

The wolf and the shepherd

A shepherd noticed that a wolf was following his flock. But as the wolf made no move to eat the sheep, he grew fond of it, and began to think of it as a guardian, not a threat. One day he had to go to town, and asked the wolf to look after the sheep.

"With pleasure," the wolf said.

When the sheepherder returned, the wolf had eaten all of the sheep.

"But what have you done?" demanded the shepherd. "Explain yourself!"

The wolf thought a moment.

"Look at it this way," he reasoned. "I did the sheep a favor, for I rescued them from the care of a foolish shepherd."

The shepherd thought a moment.

"You have a point, my friend," he said sadly.

Even in logic, half a loaf is better than none.

The wolf and the ewe

A wolf happened upon an ewe, which immediately began shivering with fright.

"Don't worry, my dear," the wolf said, "If you tell me one truth, I'll spare you."

"Very well," said the ewe. "Wolves are not to be trusted."

Enraged, the wolf devoured the ewe.

It takes two to bear witness to the truth: one to utter it, the other to turn a deaf ear.

The two young men and the butcher

Two young men entered a butcher shop. While the butcher was being distracted by one, the other stuffed pieces of snout, ears, and trotters into his robe. When the butcher noticed that the animal parts were missing, he accused both young men of trickery, whereupon the young men made an oath that they were innocent.

"Well," said the butcher, who knew the truth, "you may escape with a false oath to me, but this gets the attention of the gods!"

. . . On the other hand, the young men probably had nothing to worry about, for what self-respecting god cares a fig for pieces of ears, trotters, and snout?

The ant and the pigeon

An ant went down to the stream to drink, but was swept into the current. A passing pigeon held out a twig to the ant and he was saved. Then a fowler happened by and caught the pigeon, but the ant bit the fowler's foot and the pigeon flew off; whereupon the angry fowler crushed the ant.

Meanwhile, seeing what happened to the ant, the pigeon forgot to look where he was going, flew into a tree, and was killed.

No good deed goes unpunished.

The ant and the scarab beetle

In the summer a clever ant stored up grains of wheat and barley for the winter. When a scarab beetle asked him why he was doing twice the work of the other insects, the ant replied that the smart thing to do was to plan ahead for the winter, even if it meant hard work.

"Wait 'til winter," preached the ant, "then we'll see which of us was the smarter!"

But soon the wife of a rich farmer happened to spot the scarab beetle playing amid the grasshoppers and other insects.

"How pretty!" she said, and took the beetle home. She put it in a comfortable cage and fed it tiny sweetmeats and cake crumbs, twice the amount of food the ant had stored up; in no time the beetle became fatter and shinier. And when winter came, he congratulated himself on being much better off than the ant that had worked twice as hard and now subsisted on half the food.

Think twice before choosing brains over beauty.

The sick man and the doctor

A very sick man summoned a doctor to his house, whereupon the doctor asked what his symptoms were.

"I sweat a great deal," the man said.

"That's a good sign," said the doctor.

"And I shiver a lot," the man said.

"That, too, is a good sign."

"And my bowels are loose."

"Ah, no purgative is necessary," nodded the doctor. "Another good sign!"

When the doctor left, a neighbor happened by and asked the man what ailed him.

"How unlucky I am!" lamented the man. "I'm dying of good health!"

Thank your lucky stars doctors don't make house calls any more.

The bat, the ferret, the fox, and the owl

A bat was captured by a ferret. On the brink of death, the bat cried out,

"Oh, my friend, why will you eat me?"

"Because you're a bat," said the ferret. "And ferrets eat bats. That's in the natural order of things."

Then the bat had an idea. "But I'm *not* a bat," he said. "I'm a mouse with wings."

"In that case, I'll let you go," said the silly ferret, and the bat flew off.

But soon the bat was captured by a fox. The fox said,

"If there's anything I would like to eat, it's a flying mouse."

"But I'm not a flying mouse," said the bat. "I'm a bat."

"In that case," said the disappointed fox, "I'll let you go." And the bat flew off.

Finally a great horned owl captured the bat, and said,

"I've heard of you, my friend. You tell one person that you're not a bat, and another person that you're not a mouse. Well, if you're neither bat nor mouse, then you are really nothing, and if I've nothing to eat in my claws, then you don't have a thing to worry about."

And he devoured the bat.

A live bat amounts to nothing, but a dead bat is a dead bat.

The wayfarers and the bears

Two wayfarers happened on a bear. When one wayfarer ran off and deserted him, the second decided that he'd lie on the ground and pretend to be asleep. The bear sniffed him from head to toe and then returned to the woods.

When the wayfarer who ran away returned, the one who lay on the ground said,

"I thought you were my friend!"

"Ah, my friend, I suppose I lied," said the first wayfarer humbly.

"Oh, well, I forgive you," said his companion.

And they walked on.

Soon they encountered another bear. This time it was the second wayfarer who ran away, and the first who decided to lie on the ground and pretend to be asleep. The bear sniffed him from head to toe and then returned to the woods.

When the second wayfarer returned, the one who lay on the ground said,

"I thought you were *my* friend!"

"Ah, my friend, I suppose I lied," said the second wayfarer humbly.

"Oh, well, I forgive you," said his companion.

Finally the two wayfarers encountered a third bear. This time *both* of them ran away. Alas, *this* bear was very hungry, and he caught and devoured both of them.

Not all bears let sleeping wayfarers lie.

The wayfarers, the driftwood, and Zeus

From the vantage point of a very high cliff, two wayfarers spotted a clump of driftwood floating on the vast expanse of the sea.

"Look," one said, "a warship!" But as the driftwood came closer to the shore, the other said, "No, it's merely a cargo ship, my friend."

Finally, when the driftwood washed up on the beach, the travelers said,

"Hah! What fools we were to make over nothing in the empty sea!"

But Zeus, overhearing the insult to even the humblest part of the Creation of the gods, changed the clump of driftwood into a griffin, which promptly picked the wayfarers up with its claws and dropped them in the empty sea.

The lesson of Creation is that there's always a little something in a lot of nothing.

The man and the golden sword of Truth

In the desert a man encountered a woman carrying a golden sword. When he asked her who she was, she said, "I am Truth."

"And that's the golden sword of Truth?"

The woman said that it was.

"And what are you doing here, so far from the towns?" asked the man.

"In the old days, few men lied; but now there are lies everywhere, especially in the towns."

"But that's untrue," said the man. "Men have always lied, in the towns and everywhere!"

"*That* is true," she said, "and you have passed the test I have prepared for you. Therefore I'll pass the golden sword of Truth to you."

But the man, frightened, ran off into the desert.

Be careful when you speak the truth; someone might be listening.

The asses and Zeus

The asses, tired of their labor, petitioned Zeus to change their woeful fate. Zeus said, "I'll make your lot easier, my friends, when you turn your piss into a mighty river!" And from that day on, the asses, believing that Zeus was serious, always piss on the spot where another ass has pissed.

If you think you can make a river of your piss, you're either a god or an ass.

The ass on trial

A man decided to try out an ass before buying it. He brought it into his barn, where it immediately walked over to the fattest, good-for-nothing ass that he owned. When he returned the ass, its owner asked him if he had seen what the ass could do in the fields.

"No matter," said the man, "I have seen the sort of ass he likes to associate with!"

Don't be an ass, especially one who keeps company with fat and lazy asses.

The wild ass and the domestic ass

Poking his head through the fence of a barnyard, a wild ass said to a domestic ass,

"How sleek and well-fed you look. You're very different from me."

Just then, the owner of the domestic ass came out of the barn, placed an enormous load on his back, and beat him with a large stick to get him moving.

"Ah, my friend," said the wild ass as the domestic ass left the barnyard, "I spoke too soon."

"Yes," said the domestic ass, "but keep in mind that I receive room and board!"

In the wild or in the barnyard, an ass is an ass.

The ass, the river, and Zeus

An ass carrying a load of salt across a river slipped, and the salt dissolved and floated away. This made his load much lighter, and the ass said,

"Well! The next time I cross the river I'll slip on purpose, and I'll escape the fate the gods have decreed for me!"

It happened that Zeus heard the ass's words, and he became angry that a creature should flout his destiny thus; therefore he arranged it that the ass's next burden should be a load of sponges. And so it was that when the ass came to the river and slipped on purpose, the sponges swelled up with water, pulling him under, and he drowned.

You'll never be worth your salt by sponging off the gods.

The man, the philosophical ass, and the statue of the god

A man placed the statue of a god on the back of an ass and took it to town, where the villagers immediately fell on their knees in worship.

"Now look at that," said the ass, preening. "The villagers have prostrated themselves before me, a humble ass!"

Then the man beat the ass with a stick.

"You fool," he said. "It's the statue of the god, not you, they're worshipping!"

"Oh, well, no matter," replied the ass philosophically. "It's not who or what they see that matters . . . only how they see."

One man's ass is another man's elbow.

The ass, the cockerel, and the lion

An ass and a cockerel were drinking at a pool when a lion pounced on the ass. The cockerel crowed shrilly and the lion ran way, for it's pretty well known that lions are afraid of the sound of cockerels. But the ass, thinking that it was his bray that had scared off the lion, grew brave, and pursued the lion into the forest.

There, far from the sound of the cockerel, the lion turned on the ass and began to devour him.

"Woe is me," said the ass, "Why did I, who wasn't born a lion but an ass, set out to fight a lion?"

When you make errors in life, it's never a bad idea to blame your parents.

The fox, the ass, and the lion

An ass and a fox went hunting together. When a lion jumped from behind a bush, the fox approached him and whispered,

"I'll help trap the ass for you if you'll spare me." The lion agreed and the fox took the ass to a trap prepared by other hunters, where he fell in. Then the lion re-appeared, devoured the fox, and had the ass for dessert.

An ass is never a fox, but sometimes a fox is an ass.

The ass and the frogs

An ass attempted to cross a swamp, but he became tangled in the low-hanging thick branches of a tree. Thrashing about, he soon found himself dangling upside down over a log where some frogs were taking a lunch break.

When the ass bemoaned his fate, the frogs said,

"But we, who sit beneath you, have the good sense to stay in the swamp which is our natural home!"

Better to have your frogs in a swamp than your ass in a sling.

The ass, the cicadas, and Zeus

An ass was fond of listening to cicadas singing in the trees. He asked them,

"How is it that you have such beautiful voices? I'd like to sing as sweetly as you!"

"It's the dew," the cicadas said.

Zeus overheard this and became very angry at the ass for wanting to change his nature; so he caused a dry wind to blow wherever the ass traveled; and thus the ass waited, and waited, and waited for the dew, and finally died of thirst!

Try to change your nature and the gods will dew you in every time.

The ass and the wolf

A wolf was about to pounce on an ass. The ass, knowing he was in peril, pretended to limp about. When the wolf asked what was wrong, the ass said,

"I have a thorn in my hoof. If I were you, I'd pull it out before eating me, so you won't cut your mouth."

"Well," said the wolf, "give me your leg."

The ass gave him his leg, and as the wolf examined it to find the thorn that wasn't there, the ass kicked him hard, knocking his teeth out.

In despair that he could no longer eat, the poor wolf found a rock and dashed his brains out.

A wolf with no teeth is bad; a wolf with no brains is just pathetic.

The wild pigeons and the domesticated pigeons

A bird-catcher said to his flock of domesticated pigeons,

"A storm is coming, my little friends. I'll put you in this snare and disguise it as a shelter. When the rain starts, you must make as much noise as you can, so that your wild cousins will want to join you in order to escape from the storm. And they, too, will be my slaves."

Then it began to rain, and the domesticated pigeons made a ruckus in the snare; a flock of wild pigeons, hearing their cousins, flew into the snare and were imprisoned. They said,

"Why didn't you warn us? We, too, are pigeons!"

The domesticated pigeons replied,

"We're sorry, but we had little desire to help our cousins, if it also meant incurring the wrath of our master!"

Birds of a feather flock together, except in foul weather.

The bird-catcher and the partridge

A bird-catcher trained a partridge to lure other birds into his snares. But one day, when a traveler happened by, the bird-catcher realized he hadn't any food for their supper, and so he reluctantly decided to kill and roast the partridge.

The bird said,

"But haven't I been useful in luring my cousins into your traps? And now you wish to betray me?"

"You've already betrayed your own kind," said the bird-catcher, adding, "And now you want me and my guest to go hungry? That, too, is betrayal, my friend!"

And he killed and roasted the partridge.

If you're going to double-cross someone, get it straight.

The hen and the swallow

A hen discovered some snake eggs and decided to sit on them to keep them warm and safe. A swallow said,

"My friend, you're a damn fool to show such kindness; when those snakes hatch and grow up, they'll be the first to come after you and yours."

[Original moral]: You can't reform an evildoer, no matter how good your intentions are.

Our moral: Leave it to a chicken to improve on fouling one's own nest.

The tail and the rest of the body of the snake

The tail of a snake decided that he, not the head, would be the one to lead the snake into battle with the frogs.

The rest of the snake said, "How can you do this, my friend, when you haven't eyes or nose, like the frogs?"

"But don't you see?" said the tail triumphantly. "This way we can retreat and advance at the same time!"

[See the moral to "The widow and the servant girls," above.]

The crab and the snake

A snake and a crab made an agreement to share the same habitation. The crab was always truthful with the snake, but the snake was given to telling lies. The crab pleaded with the snake to change his ways, but the snake stubbornly refused. So one night, when the snake was asleep, the crab crept up and killed it!

Then, seeing his dead companion stretched out like a stick, the crab said,

"Well, my friend, if you'd been this straight with me before, you'd still be alive!"

[See the moral to "The bird-catcher and the partridge," above.]

The father, the daughters, and the gods

A father had two daughters, one good, one bad. He gave away the good one to a gardener, the bad one to a potter. When he visited the gardener's wife, he asked how things were going.

"I have just one request of the gods," she said, kneeling in the soil of her garden. "It is that they'll make it rain so my vegetables may grow tall."

Then the father visited the bad daughter and asked her how things were going.

"I have just one request of the gods," she said, shaping a pot at the wheel. "It is that they make the sun shine hot and bright so that my pots may dry."

The father returned to his house, and said to his wife, "If it's true that it rains on the good and the bad alike, it must also be true that the sun shines on the good and the bad alike. Therefore *I* shall make no prayer to the gods!"

And the gods smiled down on him.

[See the moral to "The man, the sparrow, and Apollo," above.]

The man and the partridge

A man captured a partridge and was about to kill it when the bird said in a reasonable tone,

"Oh, sir, if you spare me I'll lure many more partridges into your snare!"

"Why," said the man angrily, raising his axe, "you've broken the Law of Kindred, and you'll get what you deserve."

"But think, sir," the partridge said in the same reasonable tone. "Which do you prefer, partridges or revenge?"

In the end, cooler heads prevailed, and the man spared the partridge.

1. One man's justice is another man's partridge.
2. Revenge, and partridges, are best served up cold.

The thirsty pigeon and the painting

A thirsty pigeon mistook a basin of cool water in a painting for a true basin, flew into it and hurt its wings, so that a passerby was able to take it home to eat for supper.

"Woe is me," said the pigeon, "to have been brought so low by a stupid painting!"

We have truth so that we shall not perish from art. [See the moral to "The man, the lion, and the statue," above.]

The monkey and the fishing net

A monkey saw some fishermen casting nets in the river. When the fishermen went away to have their supper, the monkey scampered down to the water's edge and tried his hand at fishing. In time, however, he became entangled in the nets and slipped into the water.

"Woe is me," said the monkey, "if only I hadn't been so impetuous! Only a fool would try to fish without first learning how." And instead of trying to escape, he continued on with these self-recriminations until he drowned.

If you must monkey around with fishing nets, don't waste time judging yourself.

The dancing monkey and the dancing camel

Once there was a gathering of the beasts. A monkey got up and danced before them, and they applauded and whistled. Then a camel, envious of the monkey, got up and danced too, and the beasts applauded and whistled even louder, stamping their feet.

Shaking his head, the monkey left the gathering in a huff and returned to the forest.

There's no accounting for the taste of certain beasts.

The wolf and the well-fed dog

A wolf called through a fence to a sleek, fat, healthy-looking dog dozing in his doghouse.

"Say, friend, how did you get so plump?"

"My master feeds me quite well," said the dog.

"But what's that mark on your neck, where there's no fur?"

"That's where my iron chain rubs me," said the dog.

"Hah!" said the wolf. "I'd rather run free than be beholden to a master's iron chain around my neck."

And the wolf returned to the woods where, as it happened, there were slim pickings, and in time he starved to death.

Better to have no freedom in a doghouse than no food in a wolf's neck of the woods.

The river and the ox-hide

The river spotted an ox-hide floating down it, and said,
 "What's your name, my friend?"
 " 'Hard'," said the ox-hide.
 "If I were you, I'd change my name, for I'll make you soft in no time!"
 Not wishing to make waves, the ox-hide said, "Well, in that case, my name is 'Soft'!"
 Just then the ox-hide went over a waterfall and was torn to pieces.

Go with the flow?
Yes and no.

The clown, the farmer, and the piglet

In the ancient days, there was a clown known far and wide for his skill and cleverness. When he came to the town of Corinth, the theater was filled to overflowing with expectant crowds. The clown took the stage, remained motionless for a moment, bowed his head, and emitted the squeal of a piglet. The crowd was amazed at how real the squeal sounded and demanded that the clown show them the little animal hidden under his cloak; but when the clown opened the cloak, no piglet appeared. And the crowd burst into cheers and wild applause.

But a farmer in the audience scoffed at the clown, saying, "I can outdo him!" The next day, before the clown's next performance, this farmer concealed a piglet in his tunic, took the stage, bowed his head, pulled the piglet's ear, and out came a loud squeal. But the crowd booed and hissed, shouting that the clown's performance had been much truer to life. Then the farmer opened his tunic, showing them the piglet. "That shows you what kind of judges you are," he said contemptuously.

Booing and hissing more lustily, the crowd threw fruits and vegetables at the farmer until he was driven away.

[See the moral to "The man, the lion, and the statue," above.]

The cat-skinning contest

Once upon a time some cruel peasants held a cat-skinning contest. One began to skin a live cat with a sharp knife, but the cat screeched and ran away, and that peasant was declared a loser.

Then another peasant began to skin another live cat with a dull knife, but that cat also screeched and ran off. This peasant, too, was declared a loser.

Finally a third peasant drowned a cat and then skinned it, and he was declared the winner.

Forget what they say; there's only one way to skin a cat.

The Athenian trumpeter and the Persians

An Athenian trumpeter was captured by the Persians. The Persian general said,

"You, sir, will be put to death for fanning the flames of war against us Persians."

"But I'm the best trumpeter in all the lands," said the canny trumpeter. "If you like, I'll now kindle a fighting passion in *your* troops to help them prevail against the Athenians."

"Why, then, you shall be spared!" said the general.

By all means, toot your own horn.

The bees, and partridges, and the ploughman

Some bees and partridges, dying of thirst, asked a ploughman for some water.

The bees said,

"If you allow us to us slake our thirst, we'll fly about and chase away intruders."

"If you allow us to slake *our* thirst," said the partridges, "we'll prune your vines."

"No thanks!" said the ploughman. "I already have oxen to do all manner of services for me, as you see."

"But your oxen can't buzz or sting," the bees pointed out.

"Nor can they trim the vines," added the partridges.

"I never thought of it that way," said the ploughman, and gave them water.

Unless you're dying for a drink
Never ask a ploughman to think.

The bull and the wild goats

A bull, chased by a hungry lion, ran into a cave to save his life. There he discovered some wild goats, which lined up and began to butt him, one after the other. But the bull stayed where he was, saying,

"Never mind; I'd rather be butted by you than eaten by him!"

No ifs, ands, or butts; it's important to keep one's priorities in line.

The peacock and the crane

A peacock and a crane disputed their relative beauty. The peacock mocked the crane, saying,

"Look at my wings and breast, my friend. See how the gold, silver, and green shimmer in the light!"

"Ah," said the crane, "but unlike me, you can't fly high in the sky and touch the stars of the firmament! All you can do," he added, "is to mount your hens here on earth."

But the peacock merely laughed and strutted off.

It's easier to mount a hen than a star.

The peacock, the jackdaw, and the crane

The birds gathered to decide who was strongest and who should, therefore, reign over them.

The peacock said proudly,

"Look at my bright-colored plumage! *I* would make a splendid king of the birds."

"Yes?" questioned the jackdaw. "And what'll you do when the eagle comes to attack us?"

But the crane stepped forward and said to the jackdaw,

"Then why don't we elect the eagle king, thereby gaining his protection?"

"I never thought of it that way," said the jackdaw.

No one ever went broke underestimating the intelligence of a jackdaw.

The fox and the cicada

A fox was in the habit of lurking near a tree where a beautiful cicada was chirping and singing.

"How beautiful you are and how beautiful you sing," said the fox. "Won't you come down here, so I may see and hear you better?"

The beautiful cicada knew what the fox was up to, and said,

"My friend, I'll stay put, for the other day, when I left my lofty perch, I saw a pair of cicada wings in the dung of a fox."

1. Beware of ungrammatical foxes.
2. Keep the faith, for there's hope for us all, even in a world where foxes lurk and cicadas go slumming.
3. Always trust a cicada who knows the poop on a fox's true intentions.

The nails and the wall

The wall of a house, pierced over and over again by nails, wailed,

"Why do you mistreat me so? I haven't done anything to harm you!"

"Ah, it's not us, my friend," said the nails, "but the hammer that drives us!"

Better to be a hammer and a nail than a wailing wall.

The mule and the donkey

A mule and a donkey in the same harness learned to sing hymns to pass the time and ease the tedium of their days. Their master, upset that they spent too much time singing and too little time paying attention to their tasks, beat them both with a club until they died.

The birds that came to eat the carrion said,

"Fools! If you hadn't spent so much of your time singing hymns, your master might've spared you!"

Preach to the choir if you must, but don't waste your time on dead mules and donkeys.

The lonely owl and the recalcitrant mouse

A lone owl was in the habit of searching far and wide for some-one to talk to. He came to a mouse's dwelling and knocked on the door. He had barely begun to strike up a conversation when the mouse rudely interrupted,

"Just a minute; what're you doing here?"

"I'm lonely and wished for some company," said the owl truly, for he was an honest owl and was really quite lonely.

"Bah," said the mouse. "You're up to no good, I can see that! Well, you'll get no talk out of me! Go find a cat or a dog to converse with, if you're so damn lonely!" Then he added, "A curse on you, on your sons and daughters, and I wish you bad luck on your way home!"

And he slammed the door in the poor owl's face.

As owls would be the first to tell you, better to talk to a cat or a dog, lest you find a louse in the house of a mouse.

The wayfarers and the monkeys

Two wayfarers, one honest and the other deceitful, came to the country of the monkeys, where they were captured and brought before the oldest of the tribe.

"Who am I?" asked the oldest monkey of the deceitful man.

"You're the exalted king of the monkeys!" he replied.

"And who are these?" he gestured to the other monkeys.

"They are your esteemed chancellors and generals," the deceitful man went on.

"Good, good," said the oldest monkey, puffed up with pride. "Give this man anything he desires. He'll live in luxury with us and be like us.

"Now," he added, turning to the honest man, "Who am I and who are these?"

"You're just a bunch of stupid monkeys," replied the honest wayfarer. "A blind man can see that in a second!"

"Off with his head!" the oldest monkey cried, and the honest man, sadder but wiser, was led away.

Only the truth can make a monkey of a man.

The fox, the goat, and the well

A thirsty fox stuck its head in a well and fell in. Soon a goat happened by and saw the fox in danger of drowning.

"Say, my friend," called the fox from inside the well. "The water is wonderful down here. You ought to come down and try some!"

The goat jumped in the well, whereupon the wily fox climbed up its horns and escaped, leaving the hapless creature stuck in the well forever.

Never let a fox get your goat.

The flea and the abbot

A flea was in the habit of biting an abbot, but the abbot caught it and said,

"Hah! I've finally got you, my little friend. Do you have any last words?"

The flea said, "If you'd only open your palm so as to hear my confession, then I can die in peace."

"Very well," the abbot said; but when he opened his palm the flea escaped, laughing.

Then the abbot said to himself,

"Now I *myself* confess—to being a damn fool."

Confessor, heal thyself.

The bird-catcher and the wild rooster

A bird-catcher was sitting down to his hearty breakfast of herbs and parsley when he heard one of the cages rattling. In it he found a wild rooster, who said,

"Please don't slaughter me! I can do many things."

"What can you do for me?" demanded the bird-catcher.

"I can tell you when dew covers the wings of the birds, and when Orion sets down his bow for the night, so that you may arise and go to work."

"That's not enough," snorted the bird-catcher, and slaughtered the poor bird.

Who needs a rooster when, if herbs and parsley is your idea of a hearty breakfast, you're better off sleeping in.

The ants and the fat pig

In the summertime a colony of ants labored hard gathering seeds and grain in order to have something to eat when the weather turned cold. But a fat pig, seeing them at work, took the seeds and grain all for himself and grew even fatter.

Ants that don't make pigs of themselves in summer go hungry in winter.

The farmer and the bullock

A farmer was in the habit of struggling with a stubborn bullock. He trimmed its horns, so they would not be crowded by the yoke, thus pacifying the animal; but this strategy didn't work. Then he yoked it to a huge plow in hopes that it would teach the animal a lesson; this strategy, too, failed. He tried cajoling the bullock with quiet whispers and kind words, which fell on deaf ears.

Finally the exasperated farmer began to beat the bullock with sticks and clubs, but the bullock stamped and kicked the earth, sending many clods of dirt flying in the farmer's face.

In the end the farmer gave up, sold the bullock, and bought another.

It's one thing to piss into the wind; it's quite another to have it all fly back in your face.

The mouse, the frog, and the hawk

A mouse asked a treacherous frog to help him to cross a swamp. The frog tied a string to the mouse's leg and carried him on his back, but halfway across the frog dived deep into the water, drowning the poor mouse.

When the frog surfaced, an outraged hawk, who witnessed what had occurred, swooped down and attacked the frog; but a bramble bush, friends with the frog, caught him and pulled him down until he also drowned.

Meanwhile the treacherous frog escaped.

Poetic justice doesn't work very well in a swamp.

The wolf, the fox, and the monkey-judge

A wolf levied charges against a fox, but the fox denied that he was guilty of anything.

The judge, a monkey, said to the wolf,

"I believe that you lost what you say you've lost, though I can't prove it. As for you," he said to the fox, "I believe that you stole from the wolf, though I can't prove it."

When a monkey passes judgment, justice is served, for no one wins or loses.

The philosopher and the young man

On a Roman street a young man struck a philosopher with a stone. The philosopher dug into his pocket and took out a coin. Handing it to the miscreant, he said slyly,

"I have no more money, young man, but if you wait until the rich merchant happens by, you can hit *him* with a stone, and he'll give you more money than I!"

The young man waited for the rich merchant, and when he came around the corner, hit him with a stone. Enraged, the merchant called the police, who arrested the young man and hung him on a cross.

The only thing worse than the cross: a double-cross, of course.

The monkey and the fox

A monkey asked a fox if he could have some of his tail to cover up his bare bottom. The fox said,

"Hah! I'd rather drag my tail in the mire than pin any part of it on *your* rear end!"

Show me a monkey and I'll show you a chimp; show me a monkey sporting a bit of a fox's tail and I'll show you a bit of a chump.

The lion, the robber, and the innocent traveler

A lion, having killed a bull, sat down to enjoy his meal when a robber appeared. "I'll take some of that," he said to the lion.

"No, you won't, my friend," said the lion. "I earned this meat fair and square." And he chased the robber off.

Then an innocent traveler happened by, saw the lion, bowed, and started to walk away.

"No, no, my friend," the lion called to him. "You're entitled to an honest portion of my meat; I won't harm you, for it's clear to me that you're an honest man."

[Original moral]: This is a wonderful example of how to behave; in the real world, though, greed prevails and honesty is cheated.

Our moral: There's always room for wishful thinking, even in the real world.

The wolf, the pig, and the lion

A wolf stole a pig from a barnyard, took it into the woods, and sat down to his meal. Then a lion appeared, stole the pig from the wolf, and disappeared.

The wolf said,

"This serves me right. What is acquired by theft shall be lost by theft!"

No such high-handed sentiments occurred to the lion, who was too busy enjoying his ham dinner.

Never waste a moral on a hungry lion.

The wild ass and the boastful wild boars

A wild ass encountered a band of wild boars, who lay claim to be the most sexually potent animals of the forest. When the ass disputed this claim, they boastfully put out their members, saying,

"*Now* what do you think of our prowess?"

The ass blushed and said contemptuously,

"I could easily kick all of you with my sharp hooves, but I refuse to lower myself before such base and filthy creatures!"

Even asses know better than to kick against the pricks.

The hunter and the lion

A hunter took his bow and arrows into the mountains in search of game. All the animals fled from him except the lion, who decided to stand his ground and fight.

"Just a minute," said the hunter, stringing his bow. "First you should become acquainted with my messenger, and then you can make up your mind whether you care to deal with me!"

He let fly an arrow, which landed in the lion's rump. The lion turned and ran, whereupon a fox said to him,

"Why don't you attack this boastful archer?"

"I'm no fool," the lion said, the arrow still sticking out of his rump. "If that hunter can send a messenger such as this, just think how formidable *he* must be!"

The medium is the message.

The poor musician and the audience

A very poor musician was in the habit of playing the lyre in his closet, where the sound made extravagant echoes which pleased him greatly. Full of pride, he decided to play in a music hall, but when he did, the audience heard right away how poor he was, and booed and hissed him off the stage.

Coming out of the closet is generally a good thing, unless you happen to be a lousy musician.

The mother monkey and her baby

Zeus decided to hold a contest to determine which baby animal was the most beautiful. A mother monkey approached with her child, a flat-nosed, red-bottomed, bald and wizened little one, and the other gods laughed. But the mother said, "Please leave it up to Zeus to decide the winner. To me, this young one is the most beautiful of all!"

We've all heard that beauty is in the eye of the beholder, but this is ridiculous.

The hunter, the hare, and the horseman

A hunter killed a hare and was riding home to cook it for his supper. A horseman rode up and asked to buy the hare, but he wanted to examine it first. When the hunter gave the hare to the horseman, he spun around and galloped off without paying, whereupon the hunter gave chase. Alas, the horseman was too swift, and he disappeared over a hill.

The hunter chose to fool himself, saying, "Ah, what does it matter? That hare was really a gift."

Better to give than to deceive.

The young mole and his mother

A young mole told his mother, "I can see a bramble-berry! And I can hear it rattling in the wind!"

The mother said,

"Silly boy, you should know better than to try to fool your mother. Not only are you blind, but apparently you're deaf as well!"

Not only are young moles blind and deaf, they have no sense whatsoever.

The hungry wolf and the thirsty goat

A hungry wolf chased a goat out of the woods and into rocky country; here the goat climbed a cliff where the wolf couldn't follow. After two days, the wolf was too hungry to keep up his siege, and departed in search of other animals. The goat, too, was weak, but from thirst, and so he came down the cliff in search of water. He found a spring and drank and drank until he was ready to burst. Then he noticed his reflection, and began to admire how handsome he was.

"Ah, just look at me! I'm more handsome even than the wolf. He is, after all, quite an inferior animal."

Meanwhile the wolf had circled around, saw the goat drinking and admiring himself, and overheard what he said. Then the wolf pounced, sinking his teeth into a goat's haunch.

"Woe is me," said the goat, stiffening in his death agony. "Like humans, when a goat has too much to drink, he says things he should keep to himself."

Leave it to a goat to call water a good, stiff drink.

The lion and the ingratiating fox

The first time a fox saw a lion, he was frightened and ran away.

The second time he saw it, he hesitated, fascinated by the animal's great size and strength; still he ran away.

On the third occasion the fox had become used to the lion, and thus began to speak to him as an equal.

The lion, angered by such contempt for his status as the king of beasts, devoured the fox. Satisfied and sleepy, he lay down in the sun for a long snooze.

Familiarity breeds content.

The swallow and the gambler

A swallow, anxious for winter to end, left her home in Thebes, hoping that by the time she reached Corinth, spring would be there in full regalia.

Seeing her fly by, a traveling gambler said,

"Ah, look at that! A swallow! Spring has come at last, and now I can gamble my warm cloak and boots."

But when he reached the gambling tables of Corinth, he made foolish bets and lost both the cloak and the boots. Then, as he returned home almost naked, a snowstorm blew up, and he saw the swallow lying frozen on the roadside.

"Stupid bird," the freezing gambler said, "I wish I'd never seen you, for you were the undoing of both of us!"

One swallow does not make a spring, but it may unmake a bad gambler.

About the Author

In 2005 Steven Carter retired as Emeritus Professor of English after teaching in the university for thirty-eight years. The author of fifteen books published here and abroad, he served as Senior Fulbright Fellow at two Polish universities in 1991. He is the only two-time winner of Italy's coveted *Nuove Lettere* International Poetry and Literature Prize. Carter and his wife Janice divide the year between Arizona and Montana.